Empowering stories of overcoming adversity

Campfire for a *Woman's* Heart

Stories of Resilience from Inspirational Women

Dr Kirsty Sword Gusmão, AO
Margaret Cunneen, SC
Dr Kay Danes OAM
Liesl Tesch AM and more ...

Natalie Stockdale

With a foreword by Dr Lucy Hone

First published 2023

Big Sky Publishing Pty Ltd
PO Box 303, Newport, NSW 2106, Australia
Phone: 1300 364 611
Fax: (61 2) 9918 2396
Email: info@bigskypublishing.com.au
Web: www.bigskypublishing.com.au

Cover design and typesetting: Think Productions

Printed and bound in Australia by Griffin Press

A catalogue record for this book is available from the National Library of Australia

Author: Natalie Stockdale
Title: Campfire for a Woman's Heart: Stories of Resilience from Inspirational Women
ISBN: 978-1-922896-55-1

Empowering stories of overcoming adversity

Campfire for a *Woman's* Heart

Stories of Resilience from Inspirational Women

Dr Kirsty Sword Gusmão, AO
Margaret Cunneen, SC
Dr Kay Danes OAM
Liesl Tesch AM and more ...

www.bigskypublishing.com.au

Natalie Stockdale

With a foreword by Dr Lucy Hone

Gratitude

Thank you to everyone who contributed to this book –
the generous storytellers who kindly trusted me
with their personal journeys,
and exemplify that
'It's not what happens to you, but how
you react to it that matters.'

Thank you also to all the resilient women
who have enriched my life –
particularly my mother, Judy, and my daughters,
Sophie, Eliza and Zara.

Praise for Campfire for a Woman's Heart

Everyone experiences grief or trauma in some way. It's hard, but you never know how strong you are, until being strong is the only choice you have left. By reading these incredible stories, you can learn how these gutsy women got back on their feet. They found a way. You can too.
Lisa Curry AO

Campfire for a Woman's Heart has all the qualities of a yarning circle. Traditionally women came together to share their stories and to practise deep listening. The benefit of listening and sharing our stories is that it lightens the burden that we carry, it also gives the opportunity to learn and grow from other women's experiences.
Natalie has compiled deeply moving stories in this book, stories of strength, courage, resilience, and hope, despite all that life has thrown at these inspirational women. It is healing not only for them to share their journey but also for anyone who reads it.
Dr Miriam-Rose Ungunmerr-Baumann AM –
Senior Australian of the Year, 2021

It is my ongoing personal experience that courage is contagious – and that through the fearless and simple sharing of our own truths that we can collectively create hope and change for others around us.
Shanna Whan – Founder of Sober in the Country, 2022 Australian Local Hero of the Year, & Marie Claire's Women of the Year Advocate of the Year, 2022

In a world beset by trouble and concern, Natalie Stockdale has curated a truly inspiring series of stories that show how the human spirit is capable of overcoming great odds. With humour, compassion and uncommon sense, Natalie skilfully navigates the tricky balance of both staying true to the stories of courageous and unique acts of bravery while showing the potential for resilience and overcoming that lies within us all.
Hadleigh Fischer – Founder of Resilience Agenda & Co-founder of Mental Fitness Hub

After reading through these life stories, I am struck by the connections each woman found in the face of deep trauma and hardship. Everyone tells of starting again, rising above, gathering strength, and growing personally as a result. They show that it is not what happens to us but who we are in the process that matters. These stories will stay in your mind and touch your soul as you question the meaning of your own life's challenges.
Lyn Worsley – Clinical Psychologist and Director of The Resilience Centre

Courageous and inspiring. From Tamana Ashorzada's story of finding hope for the future despite living under the Taliban's control, to Kobe Steele's story of how orangutans saved her life after the loss of her daughter, the stories in this book are as diverse as they are inspiring.

As an author who works with trauma survivors, I know how much work goes into creating a book such as this. Natalie has compiled an array of stories that will make you cry, smile, and nod along with every page as you find the synchronicities between your story, and the many, diverse women within its pages.

Campfire for a Woman's Heart is raw, real, and honest, and the women who bravely share their stories do so with one mission in mind - to help others to transform their own adversities into flames of strength.

Jas Rawlinson – Best-Selling Author, Speaker & Award-Winning Book Coach

Praise for book one of the Campfire for the Heart series

It has been my personal experience that through candour and the simple sharing of the truth that we can collectively create hope, and change. So, I absolutely commend Natalie on this beautiful project of stories of such hope.
Shanna Whan – Founder of Sober in the Country, 2022 Australian Local Hero of the Year

Campfire for the Heart, an amazing book by Natalie Stockdale, is a book for all ages. It is inspiring and resilient. I hope this book becomes a runaway success.
Dr Arun Gandhi – Founder/President, M.K. Gandhi Institute for Nonviolence, Rochester, NY

The human brain is wired to recite and hear great stories. Neuroeconomist Paul Zak discovered that when you tell a story, your brain releases a burst of the love hormone, oxytocin. Natalie Stockdale has created the ultimate oxy-bomb within her collection of inspirational stories of resilience and perseverance. With the alarming statistics around male suicide, I'm personally grateful to Natalie for bringing the thoughts, feelings and experiences of 30 men and women, to her symbolic campfire. Thank you, Natalie.
Rae Bonney – Vice President, Australian Men's Health Forum

When we share stories, spoken directly from our heart, they can have a profound effect on those listening. The 'campfire' stories, curated by Natalie Stockdale, expose the raw vulnerability of humans, along with our capacity to conquer our darkest times. Compelling and healing.
Amber Petty – Author of This is Not a Love Song

Campfire for the Heart offers rich, diverse, and sometimes raw stories of resilience, which will inspire and perhaps guide any reader. The stories are so effective because they speak to our shared humanity, each in their own way. We are reminded, again and again, how frail we are as a species, but also how extraordinarily capable we are at surviving, and even thriving, against all odds. While some stories may resonate more with the reader than others, all have elements of grace, humility and strength. May the cup of your heart be filled with these.
Dr Jean Renouf – Founder and Chair, Resilient Byron

Campfire for the Heart provides a gut-wrenching compilation of stories where those who have encountered their worst nightmare are able to not only recount how they survived, but often how they thrived in the face of seemingly unbearable tragedy.
Dr Alexandra Wake – Associate Professor in Journalism, RMIT University

With *Campfire for the Heart*, Natalie Stockdale has assembled a broad and thought-provoking collection that shares the often-traumatic experiences of a range of remarkable Australians, including her own. Delivered with humanity, intelligence, compassion and empathy, these stories become more than a record. They form a humbling and inspiring pathway towards a way of being that is elementally uplifting, despite – and in many ways because of – being born of suffering.
Mark Muller – Editor-in-Chief, R.M.Williams OUTBACK magazine

Contents

FOREWORD 1
Dr Lucy Hone – Co-founder of Coping with Loss; Senior Adjunct Professor at the University of Canterbury, (NZ)

CHAPTER 1: STRONG WOMEN, STRONG NATION 7
Dr Kirsty Sword Gusmão, AO
Rising to my role as First Lady of Timor Leste.

CHAPTER 2: THE UNSTOPPABLE 17
Liesl Tesch, AM, MP
Rising from my broken back.

CHAPTER 3: BEYOND PORT ARTHUR 27
Coralee Lever
Rising from the tragedy that changed Australian gun laws.

CHAPTER 4: A FEARLESS LIFE 37
Dr Kay Danes, OAM
Rising from illegal imprisonment and torture in Laos.

CHAPTER 5: BLOWING THE EMBERS 47
Tamana Ashorzada
Rising from Taliban oppression and terror.

CHAPTER 6: APPLES OF HOPE..57
Regina Razumovskaya
Rising from the trauma of war in Ukraine.

CHAPTER 7: SEIZE THE DAY...67
Jennifer Butters
Rising from the loss of our son through cancer.

CHAPTER 8 : THE POWER OF FORGIVENESS..........................77
Grace Westworth
Rising from the loss of my son through surgery.

CHAPTER 9: MY ORANGE ANGELS...85
Kobe Steele, OAM
Rising from the loss of my daughter.

CHAPTER 10: THE MOST BEAUTIFUL GIRL ON EARTH 95
Amina Abaza
Rising from childhood trauma and dealing with
animal cruelty in Egypt.

CHAPTER 11: BITTEN AND STUNG, BUT NOT SHY............103
Vicki Simlesa
Rising from a life-changing injury.

CHAPTER 12: THE STRENGTH OF OUR DREAMS 113
Kate Steels
Rising from the loss of my son.

CHAPTER 13: SAILING THROUGH STORMS 125
Jacqueline Hope
Rising from a broken heart and dealing with disease.

CHAPTER 14: LEAVING A LIGHT ON 135
Suzie Ratcliffe
Rising from the loss of my kidnapped sister.

CHAPTER 15: FLYING FREE 145
Tanya Heaslip
Rising from boarding school trauma.

CHAPTER 16: SMILE AND SING 157
Sally Herzfeld
Rising to my challenges as a 1950s and 60s teacher in outback Australia.

CHAPTER 17: THE MIRACLE OF LOVE 167
Ondine Sherman
Rising to my unexpected challenges as a mother.

CHAPTER 18: MY PATCHWORK LIFE 177
Sandy Sullivan
Rising from domestic violence and homelessness.

CHAPTER 19: MY NEW YORK WAY 185
Pip Rae
Rising from PTSD.

CHAPTER 20: THE JUSTICE WARRIOR 195
Margaret Cunneen, SC
Rising from wrongful corruption charges.

CHAPTER 21: MASTER OF DISASTER 205
Sandra Black
Rising from a catastrophic cyclone.

CHAPTER 22: A FALL TO GRACE **215**
Linda Stanley
Rising, after being told I never would.

CHAPTER 23: STANDING STRONG **227**
Noelene Brown
Rising from my addiction to alcohol.

CHAPTER 24: LANDED **235**
Mia Findlay
Rising from my eating disorder.

CHAPTER 25: IN THE SPIRIT OF FLORENCE **245**
Kerry Page
Rising to my work as an international humanitarian.

AFTERWORD: **255**
Natalie Stockdale

ABOUT THE AUTHOR **267**

Foreword

Dr Lucy Hone – Co-founder of Coping with Loss; Senior Adjunct Professor at the University of Canterbury, (NZ)

In 2014, I received the phone call every parent dreads. A policeman was on his way to see us. Those 20 minutes of waiting were the longest of our lives and, when he finally arrived and told us the unthinkable news, my world tilted on its axis.

There'd been an accident. A terrible car accident. Our friends' car, which our 12-year-old daughter, Abi, had been travelling in, had been hit at speed when a driver failed to halt at a STOP sign. While the drivers of both cars survived, our beautiful girl had been killed on impact, along with her best friend, Ella, and Ella's mum, Sally, who was a dear friend of mine.

Even writing it now, it still feels surreal – the three of them dying on a back country lane, on an unsuspecting Saturday afternoon, their lives cut so desperately short, in a moment of motorised madness. It didn't make sense then, and it still doesn't now.

What I most recall from that terrible moment of hearing the news of my family's loss is an image of our lifepath splitting, like a fork in the road, forcing us down an entirely different journey, one we never saw coming and certainly didn't want. This was followed equally quickly by an utter determination to survive her loss. To keep our depleted family together. To somehow learn to live in a world without her. To live life large for my friend Sally, when she would no longer get the chance to do so for herself.

In the years since, my life has changed irrevocably – both personally and professionally – because of Abi's loss. I am no longer the mother of a daughter; all the laughter, silliness, girliness, dancing and general kookiness that female company brings evaporated overnight. Losing our tiny, skinny, radiant and bubbly daughter, I felt severed from the 'Sisterhood'.

Her premature and oh so sudden death has taught me much. As an academic researcher working in the field of resilience psychology, the irony of being forced to cope with something so huge, when I'm the one usually helping others, was not lost on me. But I also felt fortunate. Lucky to have had that training, to have sat in lecture halls learning from the best, to have dedicated hours to reading the mountain of published studies identifying the actionable tools that help people cope with all manner of hardships.

I know, for example, that resilience isn't some elusive trait only inherited by the fortunate few, but that humans are hard-wired for resilience. Instead of a fixed trait, it is a capacity that resides within us all. I know that it comes from both internal and external resources – something we often refer to as a combination of 'nature, nurture and culture'.

I'd sat at conferences and seen colleagues share landmark studies demonstrating that, when faced with all manner of potentially traumatic events, the most frequent response (as measured by scientific assessments) was in fact resilience. We have it within us to navigate life's darkest days, to keep forging forward, to pick ourselves up after false starts and bad days, only to try once more to create a life that makes sense – one we can identify with and be proud of.

What's more, I know from the studies at the University of Pennsylvania in Philadelphia, where I'd completed my masters, how possible it is to learn the skills of resilience. That these skills aren't beyond the reach of everyday people. In fact, they involve committing to ordinary processes, such as never giving up hope, approaching rather than avoiding problems, nurturing strong supportive relationships, having mentors and people to look up to, holding a strong sense of purpose, and ensuring connections to something bigger than ourselves, whether that's faith or some kind of survivor's mission.

The women telling their amazing stories in *Campfire for a Woman's Heart* have one thing in common. At their core, they personify a willingness – often it's a burning desire or bloody-minded determination – to be active participants in their life experience rather than passive victims. They are on a mission – to step up, or sometimes crawl, back into the driver's seats of their life story, to exert control where they can, to choose their response in the face of unwanted, but unavoidable circumstances.

Everything I've learnt, through both scientific study and lived experience, about resilience is evident in the stories that lie before you – astonishing stories of survival, friendship, betrayal, loss, discovery, endurance, natural disaster, hope, faith, misery, bravery, curiosity, tenacity and growth. To read these stories is to marvel at the human spirit, at its capacity to withstand and bend, not break.

Together these women demonstrate in the way they tell the stories, as much as their content, that resilience isn't about 'bouncing back' or any of that British 'stiff upper lip' nonsense. It was years before I felt bouncy again after our Abi died. Instead, you'll notice plenty of unapologetic references to bewilderment, confusion and disbelief, heartache and pain, to being scared, fearful, distraught, miserable, and feeling out of their depth. This is important. False positivity is conspicuous in its absence within these pages. Resilient people don't minimise what they're up against – there's no Pollyanna optimism here. Rather, they are pragmatic, realistic, always fully aware and ready to acknowledge how tough the situation is, but they never give up the hope that somehow, they will prevail.

Being resilient isn't about ignoring negative emotions and always expecting to be happy. In many ways, this collection demonstrates how these women learnt to live with, listen to, and learn from their negative feelings, worries, vulnerability and fears. They're not so staunch to refuse help when needed, and they recommend getting therapy or medical intervention when required. All of this is resilience too.

On a personal note, I want to thank all the women who bravely and generously shared their stories here. I have the utmost respect for each one of you, and I wish I could meet you in person to sit around a campfire and dig deeper still, to share the glow of your learnings, those hard-won understandings of what life is really about.

A special thank you also to Natalie Stockdale for putting this heart-warming book together.

With a deceased mum, brother and daughter, I sometimes worry and wonder if I've got what it takes to navigate more loss, more upheaval, more unexpected, unwanted change.

Reading these stories has put my challenges in perspective, given me hope and super-charged my belief in the power of women to comfort, support and champion one another.

I want to end by saying something about women, what it is to be a woman, to have the love and support of women, to laugh, dance and sing with women you love, who make you giggle and dribble and even wet your pants because you are laughing so hard at times. To cry with women, to hold their hands in the worst times, to coax them out of their protective caves, and to cheer them on during the biggest and smallest moments life has to offer, is such an enormous privilege.

I loved having a daughter. I will forever mourn Abi's loss, but the women in my life go a long way towards filling that void. Reading incredible stories such as those in this book gives me hope and faith for all humankind. Resilience doesn't just lie within us, but between us too. When women are empowered, their families, friends, communities, workplace teams and even whole nations are empowered too.

Chapter 1

Strong Women, Strong Nation

Dr Kirsty Sword Gusmão, AO

Rising to my role as First Lady of Timor Leste.

'When women are empowered, a nation is empowered.'

I began my life in Melbourne in 1966, as the second child of two teachers. When I was about eight years old, my father was appointed principal of a primary school, so we moved to Bendigo, a small regional city in Victoria, where we lived for the next seven years. I was blessed with a happy childhood. My parents had an interest in the world beyond our shores and a passion for social justice, which they transferred to me.

As a student of Modern Languages at the University of Melbourne in the 1980s, I met several East Timorese who had been forced to flee their persecuted, small, half-island homeland. Becoming involved in their struggle for self-determination and freedom from Indonesia's brutal occupation marked a turning point for me, one which would enrich my life with countless adventures, dangers, dilemmas and, eventually, a husband and a family in the newest independent nation of the 21st century.

My study of the Indonesian language equipped me to play a role in Timor-Leste's independence struggle. Beginning as a translator of reports on human rights' violations received from inside the country, I soon became a volunteer activist in the burgeoning pro-democracy movement within Indonesia itself.

Working undercover with the code-name 'Ruby Blade', I corresponded with and supported East Timorese political prisoners detained in Jakarta's high security Cipinang Penitentiary Institution. One of these detainees was Timor's charismatic leader of the armed resistance movement, Kay Rala Xanana Gusmão.

In 1994, I shook hands with Xanana for the first time and pretended that I wasn't particularly interested in him. Over several years, we corresponded, collaborated, conspired … and fell in love!

Our courtship was far from conventional. In fact, it was fraught with danger and hardship, not least because Xanana was serving a 20-year jail term for subversion. Therefore, the prospects for a happy life together were remote. Nevertheless, our fortunes and that of Xanana's beleaguered homeland took a positive turn years later when Indonesia's long-serving dictator, Suharto, was deposed by democratic forces.

In August 1999, the incoming President Habibie opened the way for a United Nations-sponsored referendum on the future of East Timor. The result of the referendum saw close to 80 percent of the East Timorese population vote for independence from Indonesia.

Xanana was under house arrest in Jakarta on that historic day and was released briefly to cast his vote. As a member of a small, three-person team working alongside Xanana, we organised a small, emotion-filled gathering that evening in the prison house. Our joy was tempered by a sense of foreboding, knowing that the Indonesian military and their militia proxies were planning brutal reprisals against the Timorese people for their brave choice to become an independent nation.

Three years later, on 20 May 2002, Xanana was sworn in as the first President of the newest nation of the 21st century. Being his wife, I consequently became the First Lady of an independent Timor-Leste. It was a role for which not even an advanced tertiary qualification, nor hundreds of hours of specialist training could have prepared me.

Timor-Leste was grappling with establishing the foundations of democratic governance and rolling out the most basic services to its people. Without any financial resources to support me, I decided to embark on a mission to serve the needs of the country's women.

In March 2001, I received a visit at my home in Dili from a couple from the southern coast. Their voices shook with grief as they told me their story of the death of their 13-year-old son, Carlos, at the hands of a militia leader in the turmoil that followed the 1999 referendum. Cradled in my arms, as I listened to their tragic story, was my six-month-old baby boy, Alexandre.

As if the loss of their only son wasn't bad enough, their first-born child, Juliana dos Santos (AKA 'Alola'), had been brutally abducted and taken across the border to West Timor as a war trophy by the same militia thug. Maria and Manuel appealed to me to do whatever I could to locate and return their daughter to them. Even though my husband was to be sworn in just over a year later, at the time, neither he nor I were in positions of political authority, and I had doubts that I would be able to satisfy their request.

Nevertheless, as a new mother, I felt Maria's pain acutely and resolved to do everything in my power to help her reunite with her daughter. With the assistance of friends in Australia, I managed to raise the funds required to get myself and Juliana's aunt to Geneva to testify at the Human Rights Commission. Our efforts led to the negotiation of a family reunion visit at the border town of Mota'ain in 2001. Not surprisingly, given the threats and psychological pressure she was subjected to by her captor, Juliana opted to remain in West Timor following the meeting with her parents.

What I learnt from my advocacy on Juliana's behalf led me to establish a women's organisation in her name.

In 2001, the Alola Foundation was born! Our motto – *strong women, strong nation* – encapsulates our mission to address the barriers that prevent women in Timor-Leste from enjoying their right to good health, education, socio-economic opportunities, and political participation. Underpinning *all* the work we do in the Alola Foundation is our belief that when women are empowered, a nation is empowered.

Every time I wavered in my self-confidence, or other people's expectations of me, I reflected on the privilege of being brought up in a peaceful country that afforded me a good education and limitless opportunities. With gratitude for this good fortune, I felt a moral obligation to be of service to the less privileged.

The most precious resource I fell back on to guide me as a civil society leader was my love and admiration for the East Timorese people, particularly its women. Their resilience and bravery in the face of unimaginable brutality and the world's indifference continues to inspire me. My love and respect for these people gave me a sense of purpose that is so strong, it carried me over mountains of challenges, among which were times when my life and that of my family's was threatened.

In 2008, for example, one hour after President Ramos-Horta was shot in the stomach by rebels, our house in Dili was surrounded by armed men who were attempting a coup. I told our children to hide under their beds. Xanana was away at the time, and when I called him, I could hear that he was under gunfire. Eventually, we all survived and reunited, and the coup attempt was quashed. Despite this and many other threats, my commitment to the East Timorese people has never wavered.

In 2003, I wrote a book called *A Woman of Independence*, which narrates my involvement in the liberation and rebuilding of Timor Leste. I wrote the book to not only record a passage of national history, but also to honour the people of Timor Leste – their struggles and their strengths, which continue to inspire me.

In December 2012, during one of my annual visits to Melbourne to spend Christmas with my mother and extended family, I was diagnosed with breast cancer. I can still recall gazing tearfully at the youngest of my sons as he slept, wondering whether this would be the last Christmas I would spend with him and his two brothers. I therefore found myself enrolling my children in schools near Melbourne for the next six months while I underwent treatment, which included surgery, chemotherapy and radiotherapy.

In addition to the anxiety and uncertainty I felt in relation to my health, I was racked with guilt over the disruption my predicament imposed on my children and mother, with whom we lived with for the duration of my treatment and recovery.

In the case of my health crisis, something that helped me a great deal in combating the feelings of self-pity and anxiety was practising gratitude. I focused my attention on the many reasons I had to be thankful, such as three beautiful, healthy sons and the love, encouragement and support of my friends and family.

After my treatments, I returned to Timor-Leste with a curiosity about Timorese women's experiences of breast cancer. It wasn't something that I had encountered or thought about much up until that point. What I found was sobering and brought home how lucky I had been to have had access to excellent quality medical care in fully equipped hospitals. In

Timor-Leste, the total number of women dying from breast cancer and other forms of cancer each year is unknown. Most women, particularly in rural areas, either fail to recognise the symptoms, or they are fearful of consulting a doctor if they do.

In traditional Timorese culture, acute medical conditions are often attributed to some black magic performed by an enemy or rival and hence many women rely upon traditional remedies or cures supplied by a local spiritual healer. The surgeons at Dili National Hospital told me how distressing it is for them to see women presenting with advanced-stage tumours that are inoperable. In the absence of drugs, such as Tamoxifen or strong pain killers, they often have no option but to send women home with a box of Panadol. There are no mammography or radiotherapy services available in Timor-Leste. Only the wealthy can seek medical care abroad.

With this in mind, I decided to turn my unfortunate experience of breast cancer into a positive. I established a women's cancer support group called 'HALIKU', which is an acronym for '*I choose to get better*' in the Tetum language. I gathered a group of other women survivors of breast cancer and developed a campaign of education around the importance of early detection. We trained hundreds of volunteers and health workers around the country and educated students, female members of the clergy, women parliamentarians and others on breast self-examination and the importance of early medical intervention in saving lives. In 2016, HALIKU became an official program of the Alola Foundation.

The greatest gift I acquired from my experience of becoming an accidental change-maker in the new nation was the power of listening and learning with humility and deep respect. When I first established the Alola Foundation, I thought the new organisation would focus on trauma healing, taking into account the terrible atrocities and loss that so many East Timorese people had experienced. However, in travelling around the country and listening to the priorities and special needs of women, I soon realised that what they most wanted from my organisation and me was help with economic empowerment – a small loan to establish a business, and access to markets for their handicrafts.

Women all over the country told me that being provided with the means to feed, clothe and educate their children was tantamount to having hope in the future and a better life. And this, they said, was the best and only form of healing they required. So, I put aside my own aspirations and allowed myself to be guided by theirs.

In 2022, the Alola Foundation employs over 150 staff and is one of the most reputable non-Government organisations in Timor-Leste. Juliana dos Santos, AKA 'Alola', finally fled her captor in January 2022 and lives with her parents. I continue to serve as the Chair of the Foundation, despite residing, since 2015, in Melbourne.

While I now juggle single parenthood with work for a small not-for-profit organisation and caring for an elderly mother, Timor-Leste continues to be front and centre of my world. I have days when I resent it intruding into every nook and cranny of my daily life, and then I have others when I acknowledge and embrace the fact that this small half-island is and always will be my spirit home. At the end of each day, it is my children who affirm my belief that every sacrifice involved in marrying the father of a nation was a sacrifice worth making.

To those who may be facing life challenges, I encourage you to not underestimate the power of extending your hand to others, not to distract from your own turmoil, but to help heal your soul and to propel you forward. The practise of gratitude is also a powerful healing force. Accept help from those around you, who love you, and genuinely *want to be* the hero of your journey.

Chapter 2

The Unstoppable

Liesl Tesch, AM, MP

Rising from my broken back.

'Give it a go!'

Child psychologist, Dr Haim Ginott, said that 'Children are like wet cement. Whatever falls on them makes an impression.' And that certainly applies to me.

I grew up in a family of four in a home-made caravan by a beach in New Zealand, then later in Australia. My father was anything but conventional. Although a qualified architect, he didn't like working for a capitalist society, so we were largely self-sufficient. We fished, grew vegetables, ate bush tucker and sometimes roadkill. Through Dad's modelling, I learnt that we don't have to conform to conventions; we are the architects of our lives. My mother, who provided my younger sister and I with amazing love and support, exemplified inner strength and determination.

We had few toys and certainly no technology to entertain us. We created a life for ourselves, with the meagre resources available to us. While this 'make the most of life' attitude was later tested, it has never failed me. In fact, it has propelled me into an amazing life of adventures and service to others, a life which I would not trade.

In 1988, when I was a 19-year-old university student, the front wheel of my mountain bike struck a gutter and catapulted me over the handlebars. I landed hard on a concrete driveway about two metres below, crushing a vertebra and severing several nerves. Initially, I couldn't move anything from my waist down. For the first two months, I was bedridden in hospital and told I would never walk again.

An injury is a make-or-break moment, and you need resilience and a support system to push through, or it's a tough path. Who you are prior to the injury makes a big difference to how you manage, and I am forever grateful for the resilience that my free-range childhood gave me. Equally, I am thankful for my family and friends who rallied around me during this difficult time and indeed throughout my life when help has been needed.

Over time, movement in my upper legs was restored, and I became an 'incomplete paraplegic'. With the help of orthotics, I can walk short distances, ride a bike and drive a car. When my legs tire or nerve pain kicks in, I am restricted to a wheelchair.

While it was certainly no picnic in hospital, there was lots of stimulation. The staff in the spinal unit were fantastic. They knew about the possibilities of life in a wheelchair because they were building those lives. They introduced me to wheelchair basketball, and seeing people laughing and speeding around in their wheelchairs made me realise that life in a wheelchair had potential. There were plenty of opportunities to have fun and participate in sport!

After playing basketball at school and university, I began wheelchair basketball at a local level, and as my skills quickly advanced, I found myself rising through state and national ranks. In 1990, I was selected to play for the Australian Women's Wheelchair Basketball Team at the world championships in France.

The journey with the fabulous women on my team was fantastic. We trained hard, played hard, and we all worked full-time to pay the costs. We travelled to amazing locations across Australia for training camps and competitions. As well as participating in the World Championships, we had the thrill of putting on the green and gold to represent our nation at the Paralympic Games. With five Paralympic Games (Barcelona, Atlanta, Sydney, Athens, and Beijing) under our belt, we collectively won two silver medals and a bronze medal.

My favourite Games was Sydney 2000, where thousands of school children came along to cheer us on. Sydney 2000 was the first time that Paralympians ever competed in front of packed crowds. Instead of the children asking, 'What's wrong with that person,' they would ask, 'What sport does that person play?'

This marked a major attitude shift towards people with disabilities. Those young school students are now employees and employers of the future. They saw *possibility*, not disability. The other highlight of Sydney 2000 was winning a silver medal in front of our home crowd. It was amazing.

Proudly draping my new silver medal around my neck at the after party, I was approached by an Italian player who asked me if I would like to play in a men's team in Europe. Although we had our own women's league in Australia, we were used to playing in both men's and women's competitions. 'You're good enough,' he said.

The seed to play wheelchair basketball in Europe was then sown.

Give it a go! I thought.

So, I sent my basketball resume to teams in Spain.

And not long after, the team from Alcala de Henares, a town close to Madrid, invited me to play a season professionally in the Spanish men's league.

In 2001, I packed up my life in Australia and unpacked it in Spain as the first woman in the world to play wheelchair basketball professionally.

During that time, I learnt Spanish and set up a Spanish women's team.

A couple of years later, an Italian team invited me to live in a small village on the island of Sardinia in the middle of the Mediterranean. Naturally, I said – yes!

In Italy, I bought myself a Vespa and crashed it on my first day! With greater respect for the machine, I rode my Vespa to training each day, with my one-legged flat mate, through the olive groves and vineyards and past the gentlemen picking artichokes beside their basket-carrying donkeys. On the weekends, we travelled to Roma and Milano, and after our games in Verona, the boys would stay back to drink beer and eat pizza. Meanwhile, I would wheel myself over the cobblestones, through the snow to look at Romeo and Juliet's balcony. Once again, I embraced a new language and set up an Italian women's team.

Three years later, I was invited to play for an all-women's team in Paris against all men. *Why not give that a go too?* I thought.

In 2005, I moved to Paris and had an absolute ball.

As the season was ending, I received a letter from the Department of Education in New South Wales informing me that I had a teaching job opportunity at Woy Woy. I had a tough decision to make. *Do I stay in Europe and continue living my dream, or return to Australia?*

With my parents ageing, I felt that heading home was the right thing to do. I am glad of this decision, as both my parents passed away not too long after my return.

While teaching at the secondary school in Woy Woy, I was honoured to captain the Australian squad at the 2008 Beijing Paralympics, where we won a bronze medal. In 2010, we competed in the Osaka Cup and defeated the number-one ranked American team.

I have always found that when your mind is open to possibilities, and you *believe* opportunities will come, they always do!

In 2011, an organisation called 'Sailors with disABILITIES' invited me to try out for the Sydney to Hobart Yacht Race. *That's dangerous,* I thought.

However, then came a great temptation – 'Would you like to go for a twilight sail on a 54-foot yacht on the Sydney Harbour?' Naturally, I embraced the opportunity and ended up in the 2011 Sydney to Hobart race, which became the subject of a documentary.

A Paralympic sailor, Dan Fitzgibbon, saw the documentary and asked me if I'd like to try sailing a Paralympic boat. With the benefit of sailing experience on other people's boats, I felt that sailing was a sport I could adapt to quite naturally. Consequently, I decided to … give it a go!

Before I met Dan, I re-read how to trim the jib, which is the little sail at the front of boats. However, when I met Dan and went to shake his hand, I realised he was a quadriplegic. *I'm going be trimming more than the jib!*

Our first sail together was successful, and Dan invited me to join him in a sailing regatta in Miami in the United States. Together, we formed a formidable crew on a two-person boat called a SKUD-18, designed with a 180-kilogram bulb connected to its keel, so it couldn't tip over. While I knew about sport discipline and how to trim the sails to the breeze, Dan was instinctive with the wind, tactically astute and had the patience of a saint. Plus, he knew the intricacies of competitive sailing. The initial trip to Miami resulted in three regatta victories.

Forever grateful to the sport that gave me my beautiful

sisterhood and adventures around the world, I retired from wheelchair basketball in 2011 to pursue my new love of sailing.

Instead of weekends and holidays playing wheelchair basketball, I had weekends and school holidays sailing on the Pittwater, New South Wales, and travelling the world to hone my skills. After 24 years, and eight years for Dan, we won a gold medal at the London 2012 Paralympic Games. We backed this up in Rio with another gold. However, because of the high cost of boats, sailing was gradually phased out of the Paralympics and replaced by other sports.

Over the years, I contributed to the development of wheelchair basketball around the world. Realising the social benefits that stem from sport, my girlfriend and I decided to establish an international aid organisation that uses the tools of sport for social change. In 2011, Sport Matters was born and continues to operate in Australia, Asia, the Pacific, and Africa. Sport Matters empowers individuals and unites communities, while delivering workplace health and other social messages.

Soon after, I joined the Australian Labor Party because I believed that Labor had contributed greatly to our nation, and its policies align well with my values. When a letter from our local Member of Parliament arrived, saying that she was resigning due to ill health, I had an intuitive feeling my life was going to change – again.

After extensive negotiations with local members of the Labor family, I put up my hand to become the candidate for the seat of Gosford for the New South Wales Parliament – and what a fantastic journey that has been.

When the Labor ladies joined me in doorknocking

around my community in the lead-up to the 2017 election, I felt like I had found my tribe. I was elected in 2017 in a by-election and then re-elected in 2019. I love being a Member of Parliament and see my role as an absolute privilege. Every day is a challenge to identify the problems facing my community and others across New South Wales and creating solutions to improve not just individual lives but the future of our society.

As I write this, I am heading into the next state election and find it quite hilarious that in my previous life as an athlete, I had to peak every four years. Once again, as the election approaches, I need to be at my peak, ready to win my seat and change the government in New South Wales.

The way my life unfolded has been beyond my wildest dreams. I didn't imagine that I would be a teacher, or travel the world playing basketball and sailing, but I did. I didn't imagine that I would be a Member of Parliament, and here I am.

Some people believe that luck is what happens when preparation meets opportunity. I like to take that one step further. Luck is what happens when preparation meets opportunity *plus* action. If we don't act when opportunities come, it's like standing on a jetty watching your yacht sail away. Life has presented me with amazing opportunities, and I have simply acted upon them, sometimes with fear, but always with courage.

I sometimes reflect on my life with immense gratitude because I could have lost my life. If I had the same accident in a less affluent country, with an inferior health system, I may not have survived. I am also grateful for the Australian society, which has largely been accepting of people with disabilities.

Falling (or should I say, crashing) into the world of wheelchair basketball gifted me with immense joy and a network of friends and colleagues who have similar challenges and therefore have understood the complexities of limited mobility. Once, we were young athletes with disabilities. Now, we are leaders who are committed to improving our wonderful nation for all people, especially those with disabilities.

Wheelchair basketball and parasailing have given me a voice to proudly stand up for the rights and inclusion of people with disabilities. We need to teach the world that, regardless of our disabilities, we can do whatever we want.

The most important advice that I could give people who are struggling is that *you* are your greatest strength. While other people can help you, it's up to you to take action and make the most out of your life. So, wrap your arms around yourself and give yourself a great big hug. By making a difference in your own life, you can help so many others and … helping people is the best thing you can do in the whole wide world.

Chapter 3

Beyond Port Arthur

Coralee Lever

Rising from the tragedy that changed Australian gun laws.

'I was determined to ensure that I would not let what I had lost ruin what I still had.'

I'll never forget the first time I met Dennis. It was 1960 in the Maples Department Store in Mildura, Victoria, where we both worked. When he took me home after a Christmas party, he asked me out on a date and proved himself to be a thorough gentleman. We married four years later and had three wonderful children.

In 1983, Dennis and I bought a jewellery and giftware shop in the small town of Red Cliffs. Together, we developed and operated the business, creating many friends and happy memories on the way. Dennis later developed diabetes, and in 1991, we had a major health scare with Dennis requiring two open-heart surgeries in one day!

Five years later, Dennis said, 'I've had 15 years of quality life given to me. Let's make the most of it.' So, we decided to go to Tasmania with our good friends, Ron and Vera Jary, while considering how to spend our remaining years. This was our first holiday in 15 years, an occasion we were both excited about.

Before we left, we visited our granddaughter's grave in a small cemetery in a nearby town. Dennis said to me, 'If anything happens to me, I'd like to be buried up on that hill overlooking wheat paddocks and close to Jenna Mae.' Given Dennis' fragile health, such a conversation was not out of the ordinary.

On 21 April 1996, we boarded the *Spirit of Tasmania* and began our long-awaited holiday. After six days of exploring the Apple Isle, we found ourselves in a cosy log cabin just outside Port Arthur, a historic penal settlement on the south coast of Tasmania, established in 1830 and built by convicts.

During the morning of 28 April, we headed into Port Arthur and wandered through the old ruins. They felt ghostly and cold, and I wondered how the poor men and women survived. Dennis dosed himself with insulin, and we had lunch together at the Broad Arrow Café. After lunch, we wandered down to the giftware section of the shop. Suddenly, we heard a loud explosion and dropped to the floor! After a few seconds, we stood up to see a gunman holding an automatic weapon across his body about 15 metres away.

'Don't worry, it's only a re-enactment,' Dennis told me.

'The gunman is not thinking about people with heart problems,' I said as I pivoted to walk away.

Suddenly, Dennis' hands pushed me to the floor.

This was not a re-enactment.

At the same time, Ron pushed Vera to the floor, as well as a stranger, who we later came to know as Jenny, and she grabbed my hand. I in turn grabbed Vera's hand, and Jenny pulled us both in behind a carpeted screen, where we hid.

Through a crack in the screen, I could see a lady who had been shot. Then I saw Ron, who had been shot! Vera started calling out to him as he lay dying, desperately wanting to help him. But there was nothing she could have done.

I put my hand over Vera's mouth to stop her screaming. 'You can't, you can't,' I whispered.

After about 20 minutes of terror behind the screen, quietness filled the room, and we finally crept out. Five bodies were lying against the front of the screen. Dennis' body was on the floor where we had previously been admiring the pottery only minutes before.

Staff came around to see who was still alive. They then directed us away from our husbands and into the clothing section, where we looked towards the café. It looked like a war zone. Frozen with horror and disbelief, we sat on the display boxes. The staff were amazing. Although untrained for such emergencies, they somehow held themselves together and served us cups of tea. It is amazing how resilient we humans are when we're really tested.

Because Port Arthur was quite remote, it seemed like a long time before help came for the injured people. Around 3 pm, we were taken to the Tourist Information Centre, where an off-duty police officer took the names of deceased loved ones. I called the Mildura Police Station to see if our good friend Brendon was on duty. He wasn't, so I told the officer there what had happened and asked if Senior Constable Brendon Carrodus could kindly break the news to our three children. It eased my mind being spared of having to break the news to them myself.

Around 4 pm, seven of us were taken to a workman's cottage a few hundred metres away. As a group of survivors who had lost someone, we spent several hours there with the windows blacked out and no lights, just a fire going to keep us warm. No one knew the whereabouts of the gunman, so we were all still frightened.

Believing that Brendon would have passed on the news to my children, I decided to call and speak to them myself. Little did I know, it was Brendon's weekend off, and he hadn't received my message.

Carolyn, my daughter, answered the phone. The children had heard on the radio about a massacre in Tasmania, but they didn't know that we were there. I will never forget her screaming, 'Not my dad. Not *my* dad!' I then called Brad, who was driving home from baseball, then finally our youngest son, Roy. Breaking the news to my children was one of the hardest things I have done in my life.

It seemed like a long night in that cottage – surreal.

A bus finally came at 9 pm to take us to a hotel in Hobart. Vera and I elected to stay at the Rokeby Police Academy to feel safer. We were still terrified and couldn't close our eyes, or even cry! My hearing was still muffled from the shooting. The Rokeby police kindly contacted Claudette Wells, a counsellor from Hobart, who supported us through the night.

I remember breakfast the next morning, nibbling on some toast and then ever so slowly opening the lid to the sadness I had boxed away. My family arrived at Rokeby in a police car. We held each other tightly as we cried. I gave myself permission to let it all out.

Two days later, we returned to Port Arthur to retrieve our car and clothing, which was still at the log cabin. Again, it was all so dreamlike. *Did that nightmare really happen? Can't we just rewind the clock and be back with our husbands in front of the open fire?* The cabin owners' faces were painted in shock from the news, affirming the unwanted reality.

While we had lost our husbands, others had lost their wives, mothers, children, sisters, brothers, nieces, nephews, and close friends. Indeed, there was no one in Australia who was not touched in some way by that massacre. Thirty-five people were murdered and 21 were injured in the shooting at and near Port Arthur.

The tragic event marked Australia's worst massacre in modern times executed by an individual.

The next day was my 53rd birthday. It was also the day of the memorial service at St David's Cathedral in Hobart. All I can remember is the most beautiful timber work inside the cathedral. *Dennis would have liked that*, I thought. After the service, two detectives quietly handed over Dennis' diamond dress ring, and Ron's wedding band. Dennis' ring has not been off my neck for 26 years.

I dreaded returning home without Dennis and was terrified of being alone. Brendon met us at the Mildura Airport and picked us up on the tarmac to avoid attention at the terminal. People poured into my house every day, sharing their love and sympathy. As much as I appreciated their intention, it became exhausting trying to deal with their grief as well as my own.

My children organised their dad's funeral. While hundreds lined the streets and highway, Brendon led the way in the police car to a beautiful service at our daughter and son-in-law's farm, then to the cemetery where Dennis now rests close to our granddaughter.

What I experienced in Port Arthur will never leave me. However, I was determined to ensure that I would not let what I had lost ruin what I still had. I refused to become another victim.

My external resilience resources were already in place, not for such a violent event, but for possibly losing Dennis through ill-health. We talked in depth of what would happen to me and how I would continue my life without him. In a sense, we prepared ourselves for this loss, and I think this preparation helped me to adjust to life without Dennis.

The support I received from the whole community was heart-warming. Brendon was assigned by the police force to look after me for many months following the event. He listened to me thrash out everything that I witnessed, some parts repeatedly! Brendon and his family became my second family. My counsellor, Claudette Wells, who we met in Hobart on the night of the massacre, was also a great comfort to me.

Vera and I returned to Tasmania many times over the years and always enjoyed catching up with Claudette.

Our shop was my saviour. I vividly recall wanting to get back to work as soon as possible after the event. If the absence of Dennis in the shop was a noise, it would have been deafening. But over time, it softened and eventually became the new normal. I appreciated the routine the shop gave me and the company and support of my customers.

Being an active member of the Lions Club also helped me. The Lions Club is more than a monthly social group. It's 'my tribe' and my way of life. Driven by the mantra 'together we can change the world', we act in service to our neighbours, community and the wider world. I find that when you give to other people and your community, you gain purpose, strength and satisfaction from the social connections.

For the same reasons, I enjoy being a part of the Australian Bravery Association. In 1998, Dennis and Ron received Bravery Medals for saving our lives, and I became a National Executive of the Australian Bravery Association of Victoria. I feel privileged to be in this position and wear Dennis' medal with pride at all events.

I also organise an annual, three-day reunion in Mildura for members, which unwinds with a relaxed luncheon at my home. It was uplifting when one of our new members said, 'I arrived here alone and will go home with mothers, fathers, brother and sisters.'

It's not about me. It's about what I can do to help others.

I choose not to think about the murderer and never compliment him by using his name. He is where he belongs – locked away and suffering. Out of sight, out of mind! We get to choose where our mind goes. Why would I waste my time thinking about him when I can think about the infinite wonderful people, places and projects that lighten our world?

I built a new home for myself in Red Cliffs. I didn't swing a hammer, but I oversaw every step of the building process and created something I have never done before. Every night, I sat in my favourite armchair, sipped my cup of tea, and felt proud of what I achieved. Not only was I proud of the bricks and mortar, but proud of the life I created after Port Arthur. Sometimes I feel Dennis is with me and feels proud of me too.

I kept our shop running for another 23 years and retired at 76 years of age, in 2019. In the same year, I sold my beautiful house and moved into a retirement village, which I enjoy.

When Dennis and I boarded the *Spirit of Tasmania* in 1996, we of course had no idea of the tragic events that would unfold. Thankfully, due to changed gun laws, we're unlikely to ever see a massacre like that again in Australia.

However, life is full of unexpected events – some more catastrophic than others. Be prepared for them. Discuss with your family what will happen if …. Don't overprotect your children. Let them prepare themselves for hardship too. When you're in a hard place, be kind to yourself and find a Brendon or a Claudette – someone you can talk to. Find your tribe and a way to help other people because, by consequence, you actually help yourself.

Just don't waste your life away. You are allowed to be happy.

Chapter 4

A Fearless Life

Dr Kay Danes, OAM

Rising from illegal imprisonment and torture in Laos.

'Each of us can contribute to the lives of others, and in that, we can heal from our own personal traumas.'

There was nothing extraordinary about my childhood. Born in 1967, I was a tomboy, playing army games with the boys up the road, climbing gum trees with my skinny tanned legs and racing with other children around suburban Brisbane on our second-hand bikes and paint-chipped skateboards. My long, dark pigtails flowed along behind me, reminding everyone that I was actually a girl.

I loved the colour red, and so almost everything I wore was red. There were no pink-laced dresses or silk ribbons in my wardrobe. No pretty little hats or bows or shiny pins. I was always in a hurry to get to where I was going. I didn't ever conform to the popular view that girls should walk with poise and grace and not come home with swamp mud caked three-layers deep on their elbows and knees.

Although I was somewhat of a free spirit, I did what my parents told me … well, most of the time anyway. I once told my mother that I wanted to live with 'the angels' (the Sisters of Nazareth) who walked our local streets in their flowing long white gowns. Several weeks later, I ran away to the nearby Catholic convent, Nazareth House, to be with them. Our local police eventually tracked me down, much to my parent's relief and my annoyance.

In the late 1990s, my life took a dramatic turn when, after 20 years of service in the Australian Special Forces (SAS), my husband Kerry took a leave of absence to work in South-East Asia. He was appointed Managing Director of a British-owned security company in Laos, providing security services to the international community and foreign investors.

I too had a security background and was employed as the company's Administration Manager. I also took an active role training security guards. With my connection to special tactical police, Jardine Securicor and other organisations subcontracted me to provide close protection services for their clients working throughout South-East Asia. The 1997 financial crash in Asia brought an increasing number of expatriates to South-East Asia to provide expert debt restructuring services on behalf of the major creditors and banks. Business for me was lucrative, albeit dangerous.

On 23 December 2000, Kerry was abducted by Lao secret police, who took him to an undisclosed location, in defiance of international law. There they tried to physically force him to sign a false statement against his client, Gem Mining Lao, a US$2 billion-dollar sapphire mining concession. Kerry refused and was beaten. The secret police then detained me, hoping to force Kerry's hand. It didn't.

The matter escalated into an international incident once it became known publicly that what the Lao secret police were attempting to do was illegal.

Our government and the Lao government then became embroiled in a diplomatic face-saving standoff, with each side trying to gain the upper hand. We spent almost a year in a filthy prison camp wondering if they would succeed in their negotiations.

At the time, our two children Sahra (11) and Nathan (seven) were secreted out of the country by Australian Embassy officials. They were sent home to Australia where their older sister, Jess (14), was completing senior studies because the International School in Laos only catered for students up to year nine. Jess lived with my parents and visited us on school holidays. I had no idea if we'd ever see our children after our abduction. This terrified me more than anything else.

Over the next ten months, Kerry and I endured torture, ill-treatment, and mock executions. There were many times when I thought I wouldn't survive, but Kerry constantly reminded me that we just had to. We were forced to witness the endless suffering of many political prisoners who were detained indefinitely without charge.

Inside this place they called a *death camp*, cramped in a three-by-three metre cell with five other women, I lost my freedom and almost my hope. Day after day, week after week, month after month, I prayed for deliverance from that nightmare. After three months of confinement, I was finally allowed outside my cell to exercise, thanks to some rather tough lobbying by the Australian Government and my compliance to the Lao authorities' communist indoctrination.

I'd run on the spot on top of the stinky sewage tank next to my cell block for an hour every morning, and then I'd do it again for another hour in the afternoon. While I ran, I always visualised myself in another place. I could tell you exactly the journey I was running, the people and the places I could see along the way. My mind took me far beyond the prison camp and even further beyond Laos. It was there that I ran and won my first Olympic marathon. I could actually hear the crowd cheering me on as I entered the stadium. I crossed the finish line just in time to return to my stinking cell for another 16 hours.

We knew we were innocent, and the Australian Government knew we were innocent. That's why our then foreign minister Alexander Downer sent a task force to negotiate our release – the first time an entire government had been activated in such a high-level way to get its citizens home. Yet for all that, there was no concealing how dismal the situation was for us. If our government couldn't get us out, if they couldn't find a way around the Lao government's need to save face, Kerry and I were going to find a way to get out of that stinking hole. If there truly was no hope left in outside forces, we would do everything in our power to escape and be reunited with our children.

After ten harrowing months, we were finally released to be placed under house arrest at the Australian Ambassador's private residence. A month later, we left Laos. We returned home to our three children on 9 November 2001 to face a 200-strong media contingent wanting to know why we hadn't just given in and signed the false statements so we could come home.

It wasn't as simple as that.

There were never any guarantees that we would ever go home if we did sign. And what if they just killed us after signing? What then? Is that how our children were supposed to remember us? What a horrible legacy to them.

Kerry and I are two extremely determined people who are not prepared to compromise our integrity for anything. Thankfully, we didn't have to. Our government's lobbying made sure of that.

Such life-changing experiences have the ability to alter one's perceptions. I now live by the mantra that it's not *what* we do that defines us, but rather *how well* we rise after falling. Spending almost a year in a Lao prison made me more aware of how precious life is. I now believe that we can choose to fully live our lives *without* fear, or we can live *in* fear and only half live.

I could have chosen to stay in the safety of my home,

my comfort zone, and convince myself *I have lived enough for one lifetime*; only I've never been content to sit idle. I'd much rather turn what could have been a totally debilitating experience into a reflection of strength and determination to make a difference. I've always wanted my life to have meaning and purpose.

However, after our Laos ordeal, I was constantly hindered by the debilitating effects of post-traumatic stress disorder (PTSD) and *depression.* I was prescribed medications that were supposed to make me feel better, but certain anti-depressants have serious side effects and with it, the potential to become 'accidental addicts'.

My recovery was one of the darkest times of my life. Yes, even darker than the interrogations because I had almost no control over what I was feeling now that I was free. All the effort it took for me to focus on surviving in that prison camp often meant that I had to suppress emotions such as fear and anxiety. Now, I didn't have to, and all those suppressed emotions flooded my thoughts, day and night.

At one time, I ended up in an emergency hospital room crying 'please help me'. I didn't want to die. I just wanted to free myself from my skin crawling. I frequently suffered flashbacks, night terrors and anxiety attacks. These were so intense that I could barely breathe. Kerry would wake up to find me hiding in the corner of the room. He said I looked like a deer caught in a car's headlights, totally afraid. I was exhausted from surviving.

But through it all, self-preservation, meditation, exercise and Kerry rescued me.

My life now is very different to what it was before the nightmare of Laos, although some things are still the same. I am still that same highly motivated individual with a head full of ideas on how I can leave my mark on the world. The only difference is that I have a greater appreciation for humanity and a belief that each of us can contribute to the lives of others, and in that, we can heal from our own personal traumas.

Like so many survivors, I have found that when you give to other people, you gain purpose and strength from the social connectedness. For over a decade following the Laos ordeal, I planted my foot in the human rights and social justice sectors. There I helped establish an advocacy service that directly assisted more than 1000 individuals and their families navigate foreign, judicial and political complexities in over a dozen countries.

I took a leading human rights advocacy role with the Centre for Public Policy Analysis in the United States and successfully lobbied for change on many prominent human rights issues before several US Congressional forums. For these efforts I was awarded the Medal of the Order of Australia. I completed a Master's Degree in Human Rights and graduated from law school with a doctorate.

I have travelled remarkably far from that prison camp in Laos, both physically and mentally. The resilience I gained from enduring trauma gave me the courage to help others face crisis. Since 2021, following the fall of Afghanistan to the new Taliban regime, I have contributed to the successful evacuation of thousands of at-risk Afghans, most of whom were women and girls who are now resettled in Australia. However, I am most proud of my contribution to a Senate Inquiry into Australia's involvement in Afghanistan. This Inquiry has revealed significant learnings from past failings in order to mitigate some of the risks we impose on others during armed conflicts and other complex emergencies.

My heart has done a great deal of healing. Largely because I have thrown myself back into life. Also in 2022, I travelled to the Philippines on a humanitarian mission funded by Rotary International and a US charity called Florence Nightingale Global Health. There our team coordinated more than 100 life-saving cardiac surgical procedures to children who would otherwise have died and conducted several major dental clinics. I delivered mental health first aid training to hundreds of health professionals, local community counsellors and teachers, to educate them on how to break the stigma of mental illness, which is impacting the lives of millions of Filipinos.

In imagining the world being a better place, many lives have been transformed. We came together as like-minded people with a passion for humanity – people of action! From that, we made a difference to the lives of others.

The most important advice I could give anyone struggling to regain their mental health is to seek professional help early. The earlier you find appropriate support, the greater the chance that you can stop small problems from becoming bigger ones. The road to recovery can be a long and difficult one, but if you can learn to let go of that fear from past traumas, you diminish its power over you, and then you will be in a position to embrace whatever the future holds.

I let go of the idea that the life I had planned was the only one I could have. Only then did I discover that life is so much more than I ever imagined – a series of great adventures!

Chapter 5

Blowing the Embers

Tamana Ashorzada

Rising from Taliban oppression and terror.

'When I find freedom again, she will not be taken for granted. I will honour her through a big, brave and rewarding life.'

There is one thing the Taliban cannot strip from us – hope. For without hope for freedom, we have nothing. While hope may look like a tiny amber glow in a warm chip of coal at the bottom of a cold pit, we continue to blow the embers – softly, invisibly.

Before the Taliban seized control of Afghanistan in 2021, my family lived in Kabul. My father passed away with an illness in 2018, leaving me, my mother and two brothers together at home. My three older sisters were married and lived nearby with their husbands.

Born in Kabul in 2000, my life as a young woman in Afghanistan was devoid of many of the freedoms enjoyed by most women beyond our borders. In my country, married women couldn't go to school or university, and workplaces for women have never been safe. Our culture has always been 'about men', while women feel fear to a small or great extent.

As a girl, my future goals would constantly change. I wanted to be a pilot, a journalist, or a doctor, but when I was 16 years old, I aspired to be an actress and play hero roles. Through acting, I wanted to show that women can be whoever they want. One of my favourite actors is Angelina Jolie. I not only admire the strong female roles she plays, but also her humanitarian work. I also remember enjoying the movie *Charlie's Angels* for the same reason – strong women who could do whatever they wanted.

My dream to be an actress, however, was top secret because my mother wanted me to be a doctor. I delayed disappointing her for as long as possible, until the day I passed my examination that was my key to Kabul University and the study of theatre. Shortly afterwards, Mum noticed how much I enjoyed my course (and social life) and was happy for me.

My brothers and sisters were also supportive and encouraged me to reach high.

At the same time, we all knew that being an actress in Afghanistan wouldn't be easy. Most families don't encourage their daughters to work in any capacity in film or theatre. Women in the acting industry are stigmatised, and most families object to their daughters working with 'unholy' men, who are not Islamic.

Kabul University had a grand theatre hall. I remember acting in Shakespeare dramas and once playing the role of a villain. Such moments were the happiest of my life. There was something about being on a stage and entertaining people that made my heart full. It felt 'right', what I was born to do.

Having always been interested in women's rights in Afghanistan, my radar was switched on for ways to help them. To that end, I worked voluntarily for a Civil Rights Investigation Organisation in Kabul. My colleagues and I would collect and collate information about women rights and petition for women whose rights were violated, which often occurred in workplaces, including the army.

It might surprise you to know that we used to celebrate Women's Day once a year. On this day, mothers, sisters and friends would get together and celebrate being women. We'd enjoy a special cake, drinks (alcohol is forbidden) and biscuits. Some men would buy gifts for their wives, play music and take photos of the occasion. We also acknowledged Women's Day at school and studied topics about women – inspirational mothers, women's rights leaders, and female characters in poems and books. There are many illiterate women in my country, so on these days, they would come to school, and we would share our learnings with them. We all loved these days for, back then, the fire of justice and equality for women was glowing with strength and confidence.

So, while it was far from perfect, my pre-Taliban life was mostly good. I had a great family, social life, rewarding work and was studying a craft of my choice. My life, and that of other women in Afghanistan, was full of hope.

Then, on 15 August 2021, the curtains on that world closed. That morning, I dressed for another day at university. My friend Shahida called and said, 'Have you heard? People are saying the Taliban are in Kabul!'

What does this mean? What do we do? I thought.

My brother then called me from his office. 'Stay at home,' he said. 'It's not safe outside. The Taliban are everywhere.'

The sun was shining outside that day, though in my heart, it was dark, the darkest day of my life. Freedom was gone, yet it was hard then to comprehend what that really meant.

The day turned into night – the night the Taliban celebrated their control with gunfire. Thousands of bullets were wildly shot into the sky for hours. While the Taliban were revelling in their power, they were sending a clear and loud message to Kabul that they were a highly weaponised and formidable force.

My mother closed our windows and told us to keep far away. Bullets were ricocheting and dropping everywhere from the sky. The Taliban's shooting party wasn't to be a 'one-off' event. On New Year's Eve (which we celebrate in March), they had another spree. Sometimes, they even shot the sky on random nights, and whenever they did, we held our breath and hoped no one would be hurt.

Most old houses in Afghanistan have bathrooms outside. My friend's mother, who was washing her hands in her backyard one night, was struck by a bullet on her chest. She was rushed to hospital and fortunately survived.

In the days following the Taliban seizure of Afghanistan, information about the *new rules* flowed into our home. Girls couldn't go outside without a man. Women couldn't go to their jobs. If a woman left her house without a hijab, she would be beaten with whips. Men and women couldn't even be together at the same place. This included on buses and at bus stops. If a man came along, I had to leave the bus stop! And it continues to this day ....

In September 2021, the Taliban closed the Ministry of Women Affairs and all organisations involved in women's rights, including ours. Women and girls who were brave enough to protest faced gunfire from the Taliban in the Kabul streets. I wanted to join these brave women in their fight, but my mother didn't allow me because she knew it would be violent.

While it was all terrible news to grasp, I found the closure of Kabul University particularly hard because I understood the consequences of this action. Women wouldn't be educated. Women would be disempowered. I was not only devastated about the impact of this on my life, but on the lives of my Afghanistan sisters and daughters. The disadvantage this presented to future generations.

Nelson Mandela said that 'education is the most powerful weapon we can use to change the world'. By stripping girls and women of education, the Taliban create a population of ignorance, which is easier to manipulate. Ignorance allows leaders to fool people and bad administrators to maintain control.

Our family has been fragmented by the Taliban in many

ways. My three beautiful sisters, who were also my best friends, left Afghanistan with their husbands in late 2021. My mother and I don't know if or when we will see them again, and we miss them every day.

In 2016, my brother, Hadi, was on duty as a military officer in the Ghazni province. He loved his job, protecting his home and country. He particularly enjoyed the comradery he shared with the other soldiers. One day, he didn't come home. A rogue Taliban shot him.

Now, there is only my mother, two brothers and me. Like most women, my mother is a housewife and stays at home, constantly worrying about her children's safety and future. If I am one minute late home, she calls me and asks, 'Why are you late? Are you ok? Where are you?' She does the same with my brothers because she knows from experience that whether you're a man or woman, the Taliban are dangerous. Despite her well-founded fear, Mum continues to support us to do and be our best.

My older brother – who discontinued university when Hadi died, to support our family – has his own business. My little brother, now 14 years old, is going to school. I am lucky because both of my brothers object to female oppression and treat my mother, sisters and me with love and respect. In a culture where brothers and sons discourage their female kin to work or study, my brothers are exceptions.

My teachers at Kabul University fled Afghanistan when the Taliban struck. Just as they vanished, so did my hope of continuing my acting course there. So, what were my options? I could stay at home and be a housewife like Mum, or I could go to a private institute for nursing and midwifery training.

While nursing wasn't a career I ever imagined or wanted for myself, it was better than staying at home and fretting. So, my life now consists of going to the nursing institute, in full black attire, then returning home. Coffee, walks in the park with friends, training in the gym, wearing colourful clothes, are distant memories of the past.

Now, the Taliban are ubiquitous in Kabul. They have no uniform and have mandated *all* men to grow long beards. They all look the same. Danger is anywhere and everywhere.

One day, when walking back home from the nursing institute with my classmate, we saw a Taliban furiously beating a man on the street with a whip. The man tried to escape but was dominated by a second Taliban who came along, accused him of stealing and told him that he was to be punished. There was nothing we could do to help the poor man. I thought about his wife, children and mother and how they would worry about him if he didn't make it home.

Another day, just outside the institute, an armed Taliban stopped a girl and yelled at her because her dress was too short. Frightened and humiliated, she turned around and, assumably, returned to her home. Like oxygen, we breathe fear every day. Whether it be anxiety from accidentally being somewhere with a man at the same time, or from the horror of witnessing an attack – fear is ever present.

Greater than fear, however, is courage and hope.

One of the few things we are still allowed to do is read. I have read more books since the Taliban took over than I had in my 20 years prior! I can't go to bookstores, but I can download them from the internet and read them digitally. I particularly love reading memoirs of women who have triumphed over adversity.

There is one book that stands out to me as my prime inspiration – *I Am Malala*, written by Malala Yousafzai, who was shot by the Taliban in Pakistan while she was on a bus. With surgery in the United Kingdom, Malala survived and, through her memoir, taught me to keep learning and holding onto hope.

Malala advocates equal access to education. 'Let us pick up our books and our pens. They are our most powerful weapons. One child, one teacher, one book and one pen can change the world.' She also talks about the innate power of women, despite our oppression. 'There are two powers in the world; one is the sword and the other is the pen. There is a third power stronger than both, that of women.'

While the doors of universities have closed to women, some of us (the lucky minority with a mobile phone or computer) can educate ourselves in other ways – digital books and videos from YouTube. The problem is, however, the exorbitant cost of the internet. Afghanistan is a third-world country, and my people struggle to earn enough to pay for three meals a day. Internet access is a luxury for which I am grateful.

Through self-education (and my nursing training), I feel like I'm moving forward on a stream. Courage and hope are carrying me. I don't know where the stream will take me, but the alternative is staying at home in a stagnant pond, paralysed by fear. By moving forward, ever so carefully, I feel each day is one day closer to freedom.

I don't know where freedom will be, for she is gone from my country. My sisters, teachers and most of my friends have left Afghanistan to find her, and I want to leave too. Like every woman, I want to choose what I wear, where and when I go, who I hang out with, what I study and aspire to be. I want to live without fear in a peaceful place where men and women are regarded as equal. Then, from a place of safety and empowerment, I will help my mum and other Afghanistan women.

If courage and hope are two legs on a chair that hold me, the third leg is trust. I trust that I am on a stream that will flow to a good place, the right place, where I can achieve my dreams and, in turn, help others to achieve theirs. I do my best to move forward, and at the same time, I surrender to whatever forces are at play that determine my destiny.

The fourth leg on that chair which sustains me is gratitude. Gratitude for my family – my sisters and brothers, and especially my mum, who is my champion. Mum has suffered a lot of pain losing her son and husband and is now distant from three of her daughters. However, Mum encourages me to never give up. I hope that one day she'll be proud of me.

The Taliban want women to stay at home and be small. But what they have inadvertently taught me is to live BIG! Everyone, men and women, has a future to reach for and, my gosh, when I find freedom again, she will not be taken for granted. I will honour her through a big, brave and rewarding life.

It is not important how bad a situation may be. What is important is how we deal with the situation. Even under a tight and sometimes terrifying Taliban regime, we get to choose if we stay in a putrid pond or gently flow along a stream towards our dream. Life is precious. Find your stream and guard your dreams.

BotanicMarket

Chapter 6

Apples of Hope

Regina Razumovskaya

Rising from the trauma of war in Ukraine.

'When you face war directly, without the theatrical stuff, all your plans and dreams are ruined in a second, and you know that your life will never be the same.'

In 2021, I woke up beside my second husband in Kiev, Ukraine, with a sense of comfort that my worst life experiences were over. I thanked God for all the hardships and challenges that I'd gone through, because if it weren't for them, I wouldn't be where I was.

In fact, on that day, which was my 43rd birthday, I recognised one particularly important thing. You can't tell if something that is happening to you is bad or good (even if you seem sure about it) until you know where it leads you. I have stepped back and thought about each 'seemed-to-be-negative' event in my life and understood why I had to overcome them. I felt my hands tingling as if all my body energy screamed with joy at this revelation. What a birthday gift!

Divorce from my first husband was painful, followed by a disastrous second partnership that ended in betrayal, physical abuse, money theft, the loss of an unborn child, and desperate loneliness everywhere in between. Dealing with loneliness was one of the toughest challenges I've faced. Without a close connection with other people, I felt meaningless, dispensable, a nought. I was lucky to have friends who helped me to fill the silence on weekends, but nobody could fill the deep void left by the absence of my partner.

However, my earlier life wasn't all sad. I had a great career, and my first husband was smart, charming and caring. He helped me understand who I was and what strength I was capable of. Although we lived in Russia, we created wonderful memories travelling the world. It wasn't meant to be a forever relationship, but my love for him was so strong that it was worth preserving the memory.

I now recall with gratitude that period when I was left alone with no partner and had lost hope of creating a new family.

Many must be aware of this feeling, when you are worn-out, your life is broken apart (at least you think it is), and you don't want to get out of bed in the morning, or you start crying for no reason.

But then, something changes. You decide: *enough – I'm not going to live like this anymore.* And you step out of the darkness and into the sunshine.

As soon as I decided to take charge of my life, I created a vision of my desired future. With pen and paper, I described the life I wanted on the left-hand side and scribbled pictures on the right-hand side. I have kept these pages as a record of those times. At first, it was difficult and seemed like nonsense, but I disciplined myself to dream. Gradually, I immersed myself in the game. It became fun, and my thoughts shifted from, *this is impossible*, to *this might happen*, to *this IS my future!*

Finally, I turned my imagination to action. I began exercising, dining out with friends or acquaintances, attending different workshops and even put braces on my teeth! I returned to my extreme hikes, an activity I enjoyed as a student. I spent a month with a small tourist group in Kamchatka, Russia, exploring volcanoes, living in a tent, boating and campfire cooking. When I returned from this trip, I was alive with vitality and optimism. In such a state, there was no room for negative thoughts, which I had previously harboured. They were gone!

One month later, I had a coffee while chatting with a stranger at the airport on my way to Barcelona. Later, he became my husband. Do you think it was a coincidence? It wasn't. I prepared myself for good things to enter my life, and they did.

By the age of 40, I was empowered by the lessons of my earlier problems and ready to embrace a happy new life with my new husband in an exciting new country – Ukraine. I was born in Russia and lived there all my life before I married Volodya in 2014.

Volodya is from Donetsk, Ukraine, and we decided to move to Kiev, for a fresh start. It wasn't easy. Aside from the cultural and language barriers that I personally faced, Russian military aggression in 2014 destroyed Volodya's house and most of his business in Donetsk. His house was robbed by marauders, and his beautiful nursery was bombed. At that time, I became pregnant with our first child and therefore wasn't much help.

It was an enormous loss and a great injustice, but we were just two of thousands of other Ukrainians who lost their assets. Many others, of course, also lost their friends, mothers, fathers, brothers and sisters. The only way of coping was to accept what we couldn't change and begin from scratch.

We established a new plant nursery business, rented accommodation and finally built a house of our own on the premises of our garden centre. It wasn't our dream house, but it was cosy, and we finally felt 'at home'.

Our first warnings of the second wave of the war came at the end of 2021. It seemed so incredible, that we could hardly believe it! Sometimes, people around us would talk about it, trying to make sense of the threat, to figure out if they had missed something. Then we saw the news on television that the aggression would start on 16 February. Kiev stayed awake that night. Volod and I sat close to each other on the couch, with our now two daughters asleep on our knees.

The war didn't start, and as the sun rose that morning,

we reassured ourselves that it couldn't have started anyway, because … it just couldn't!

Eight days later, on 24 February 2022, we were woken by our house shaking from the bombing attacks. I had a gut-wrenching fear as I looked at our frightened girls and didn't know what to do. War entered our lives. When you read books or watch movies about war, you don't realise what it's like because you're in a safe place. But when you face war directly, without the theatrical stuff, all your plans and dreams are ruined in a second, and you know that your life will never be the same.

As a mother, you try to shelter your children from war, fear, and any abuse. You understand that starvation is a realistic possibility when you see near-empty shops within just one week of war. Thank God, I always kept a lot of food in stock, so we managed it for a week or so. When our provisions were depleted, we started to eat junk food, which was all that was left in the shop. My husband, just once, managed to buy two chicken eggs, a frozen pizza and a duck's breast. A friend had some flour and made us a loaf of bread. That was our ration to last us until … we didn't know.

On the next day of attacks, we moved to a bomb shelter. At first, we were instructed to go there at night and then spend the day at home. Then, at the start of the second week, many people moved to the bomb shelter full-time, as it was unbearable to stay at home with the sounds of air sirens and distant explosions.

In the bomb shelter, I felt like we were hunted animals, stacked upon each other with hundreds of others in a basement. There were women with newborn babies, old people who could hardly walk, hundreds of children and teenagers with their mums, some military guys ... all kinds of people. Each family had up to two square metres to use. All the men were on day and night 'watch' around the district for enemy sabotage groups.

War is not only about military actions. It is also about people's behaviour. You might be injured, or even killed by surrounding people in panic. War makes all of us inadequate and releases all the bad and evil – people fighting fiercely at gas stations, women fighting over the last packet of sausages. Volodya was threatened by armed men when he insisted on keeping the emergency exit of the bomb shelter open.

Three weeks in the bomb shelter made me another person. I re-evaluated a lot of things that I had previously taken for granted. For the first time, I understood the full meaning of freedom. Freedom to not be afraid all the time. Freedom to see daylight. Freedom to have a peaceful sleep, a nice cup of coffee in the morning. Freedom to keep my family safe.

Was I depressed, overwhelmed, and defeated? Not at all. With our inborn survival instinct to be free, all I wanted to do was escape and start a new life with my family.

In March 2022, Bucha was massacred by the Russian troops, escalating the urgency to flee from Ukraine. Because Volodya had more than three dependent children (with another daughter from his previous wife), he was exempted from war duties. So, with one suitcase and just enough fuel to reach the border, we started to drive through the country. I remember Volodya instructing me to take only essentials and some food for the children. All our other belongings were left behind, probably for good.

Two sleepless nights passed before we reached the border. All I remember is an endless chain of military checkpoints with armed men stalking around our car, checking all our belongings, who was inside, and our documents. During the curfew hours, we had to stop at a village, or risk being taken as an enemy and being shot on the road.

As luck would have it, my eldest daughter broke out with a severe case of chickenpox. She had a high fever and was itching all over. I couldn't help her with a soothing cream or a comfortable bed. We just had to keep moving. The trip was fraught with danger, and I remember distracting our girls with lots of chips. One of my greatest fears was running out of fuel … and chips!

We were passing through a village when we saw a man holding a sign: *Stop and have a snack. No money needed.* I didn't believe my eyes and asked him if it was true. He reassured me that he did indeed have food to share with us.

That was the best soup I had *ever* had and the best *pirozhki* with meat and vegetables. It may seem like a small act of kindness, but to Volod and me, it was an act that will remain etched in our hearts forever. Upon leaving, our girls were presented with a bag of juicy apples. I smelled the sweetness of the apples and new hope for freedom.

After three days on the road, we finally made it to the Moldova border. Crossing the border felt like winning a lottery ticket for another chance to live. We were lucky.

For the following three weeks, we traversed several countries and locations, trying to figure out what to do. An Australian friend, John, had written to us just before the war, inviting us to 'get on a plane and come to Western Australia. With love from Down Under'. His message kept me afloat. Somebody was waiting for us, so we should get there, we hoped.

At the end of March 2022, we received our Australian visas and flew to Western Australia.

Here we are now, in one of the safest places in the world, at the precipice of something new. Yes, we are refugees, with no home of our own, no business to earn money, not even a car to drive. But we have a chance to live a new life. I'm not frightened, but I'm curious to know how our new life will unfold. The mystery of it thrills me. While I am concerned about our girls – how they will adapt, how will we create a good life for them – my resolve to succeed is strong. We have started from scratch before, and we can do it again.

My greatest challenge currently is my relationship with my family in Russia. Can you imagine a case when your mother, father, brother, and most of your dearest friends are on the other side of the war, supporting those who have ruined your life and millions of other people's lives? Such is my situation. Brainwashed by media propaganda, my family are blind to the destruction caused by Russian leaders. They refuse to realise that the Russian troops are torturing and murdering civilians and marauding homes and property. They are even trying to convince me that Russia wants to establish peace and goodness in my country.

I can only see one way out – to disconnect. I can't tell you now if the decision is right or wrong, or if I can find enough strength to forgive them one day. The situation is too raw, too new for me to find the answer to this question. So, Volodya, Yeva and Maiia are my only family for now.

I am grateful for all my life experiences, without exception. They have given me confidence to overcome fear and be the creator of my future. We can all create the future we want, despite disappointments and disasters that may seem catastrophic at the time.

Create a vision of the life you want. Draw it, scribble it, write it, cut and paste it. See, smell and feel your dream as though it's real. Then, take action towards it. If it seems overwhelming, just take one step, then another, all the while suspending disbelief. By doing so, you prepare yourself to attract what you want.

While the trauma of war in Ukraine was (and still is) terrible, I maintain that I felt most vulnerable when I was lonely, earlier in my life. The difference between the challenge of war and immigration, and my earlier challenges, is my family. Volodya, Yeva and Maiia give me meaning and purpose. They transform the 'I' to 'we' and give me strength and motivation to endure anything. I've learnt the importance of relationships. Do not isolate yourself. Connect with other people, whether it be a partner, friends, family, or social networks. Transform 'I' to 'we'.

The couple who gave us a meal and apples when we were tired and hungry affirmed to me the importance of kindness. Kindness is a gift we don't keep for ourselves. We pass it on, and it revolves around the world. Receive kindness graciously, then pass it on.

Chapter 7

Seize the Day

Jennifer Butters

Rising from the loss of our son through cancer.

'It is so often that through adversity, we are challenged to make a difference.'

Prior to Nicholas' diagnosis, we were a busy, child-centred, organised family living in the Hunter Region of New South Wales. As a physical education/personal development teacher, I enjoyed my work in a large local high school. We thought our life was complete with three beautiful, healthy sons – Coen, Nic and Alexander. Like all young, active boys, they would chase each other in the yard, kick balls, swim and play games.

Nic loved kindergarten and would bound through the gates with his packed lunch, shiny shoes and beaming smile, ready to laugh and play. Three months into the year, his enthusiasm was halted by nausea, vomiting, colour draining from his face.

'Looks like a virus,' we were initially told.

As the symptoms lingered, we took Nic to hospital where he was diagnosed with an obscure infection – nothing that a course of antibiotics wouldn't fix! Headaches and sensitivity to light, however, heightened our concern, so back we went to hospital for more tests. As the doctors investigated Nic and held hushed conferences, I felt (in my naivety) a confidence that illness wouldn't touch my family.

They took Nic for a CAT scan for possible meningitis. I was worried, of course, as it's a terrible disease, but I consoled myself in knowledge that it was treatable if detected early.

When a group of 'important-looking' doctors entered the room, I felt sorry for the family of the sick child they must be attending.

However, I heard the doctor call out, 'Craig and Jennifer Butters', and I immediately thought, *no, no, not us!*

Our world suddenly turned in slow motion.

Bewilderment, confusion and disbelief permeated my soul. Heartache and pain filled my being. We were shown an x-ray on a screen, but the word *medulloblastoma* was incomprehensible. Then came the words that shattered our world and changed our lives forever.

'Your son has a brain tumour.'

Days later, Nic began his battle with eight hours of surgery.

At this stage, Coen was seven years old, Nic was five, and Alexander was two. It was hard telling the boys that their brother had cancer. Coen was optimistic. 'Nic will be fine, Mummy,' he said. Alex was less sure how to respond, but Craig and I were determined to maintain a 'normal' family life as much as possible.

I took leave from my job to care for the family. I spent the days in hospital with Nic, returning to my parents' home to cuddle Coen and Alexander before they went to sleep at night. Craig spent the nights with Nic in hospital. We made an invincible team! With the support of family, friends and the staff at the John Hunter Hospital, we emerged from the first phase as a stronger, resilient family, awake to the fragility of life.

For nine years, we were thrust into a new world of medicine – surgery, radiotherapy, chemotherapy, vincristine, etoposide, clinical trials, topotecan, portacath, stem cells. We learnt a new language and, with hours of study attached to each new word, we researched treatments around the world in a desperate attempt to save him. On borrowed time through gruelling chemo and radiotherapy treatments, we lived in hope of a future cure. Hope carried us forward.

While the surgeries and treatments wreaked pain throughout Nic's body, they didn't dampen his zest for life. Nor did the oxygen bottles that were attached to him. Nor did the relapses, which occurred five times.

In 1998, when we heard the dreaded words again, 'Sorry, I have some bad news,' Nic bravely said, 'Don't worry, Mummy, you'll be fine.'

Nic's indefatigable courage, sense of humour, self-confidence, and true engagement with all those he met enabled us, as a family, to overcome the seemingly insurmountable challenges.

As we fought for Nic, we strengthened as a family. Our son, who was fighting for his life, opened our eyes to what really mattered. He taught us to listen, to laugh, to cry, to trust, to give, to capture the moment. 'Seize the day' became our family mantra.

In 1999, I was inspired to write the following poem:

NICHOLAS

They say children with life-limiting illness are special.

Their strength supports those who would like to fall.

Their love touches our hearts.

We need only to meet Nicholas to feel his warmth,

He doesn't ask us to carry his pain.

His gentleness, kindness and trust carry us away from our own self-pity.

Nicholas has taught us many things.

To take time to appreciate the beauty around us, enjoy the moment.

The spontaneous kiss, and I love you, Mummy and Daddy.

Nicholas enriched our lives in so many ways.

To have shared his life is the greatest gift of all.

While we attempted to keep life as normal as possible for the three boys, we wanted to provide opportunities to build precious family memories that would last forever. Whenever Nic was well, we travelled and bottled every moment of joy with love and gratitude.

Running also gave me solace. Each morning before the sun rose, I would rise and run. Wherever we travelled, I ran. Running was my time-out. It nourished me in my darkest days and strengthened my mind and body.

Nic fought so hard to survive, yet, nine years after the diagnosis, he said, 'Mummy, I can't fight them anymore.'

On 8 December 2004, Craig and I lost our beautiful son. Coen and Alex lost their brother. We miss him every day.

Nic's final 21 days were particularly distressing. In a loud, busy hospital, devoid of privacy, other children were coming and going, some were visitors, some with hope for a cure. Laughter would bubble down the corridor, while we were quietly grappling with the fact that our beloved child wouldn't be going home.

In his final few days, our immediate and extended family and his many friends didn't have a quiet, sacred place to spend time with him, to say goodbye, or build final memories. There was no room for Nic to pass away with the dignity his life deserved.

We recognised the need for specialised facilities for dying children, and support for their families. We realised that while adult palliative care was well established and delivered, nothing was available to meet the quite different and complex needs of dying children and their families. The Ronald McDonald House provides separate accommodation for families while their child is in hospital; however, the ability for family and friends to stay with a terminal child in an acute treatment setting wasn't available.

After emerging from the loss of Nic, we had a choice: to hibernate in heartache, feel bitterness and anger, or find strength and purpose through empathy and provide support for those who find themselves travelling a similar road.

Every day, on average, one Australian family is delivered the news that changes their lives forever. Four hundred children in the greater Hunter Region of New South Wales suffer a life-limiting illness and will require hospitalisation. Fifty of these children will die this year.

While we couldn't save Nic, Craig and I were able to help children like Nic and their families, and that is what we decided to do. Determined to enable sensitive care in a supportive environment to the children in our region with life-limiting illness, we founded the Nicholas Trust in 2008. Nic, we thought, would like us to do that.

Our vision was to develop a space where complex medical equipment was, as much as possible, blended behind the scenes to facilitate a modern comfortable home-like setting with a separate parent bed, kitchenette and shower. The Nic Trust gained momentum through an advisory board of committed volunteers, all of whom were high-achieving individuals in their own field. We were extremely fortunate through word of mouth to find ourselves with a 'dream' board consisting of a businesswoman of the year, a barrister, paediatric doctors, an advertising executive, a forensic accountant, and a commercial architect, all of whom provided incredible guidance, insight and services at no charge.

We are proud of what the Nicholas Trust has achieved. In conjunction with our partner organisations, we have raised more than 1.5 million dollars, with 100 percent of the funds distributed to paediatric palliative care. We have successfully advocated for a dedicated paediatric palliative care service, which delivers support to children, young people and their families in the Hunter, North Coast, and Northern New South Wales Health district. It cares for small, frail newborn babies through to chronically ill adolescents; those with special needs due to degenerative muscle conditions to those diagnosed with cancer. These children spend many weeks hospitalised and receive the best of care by this devoted team.

We have financed the construction, within our regions' hospitals, of seven dedicated rooms for families to be together, to grieve and gather strength. The rooms provide comfort and privacy to families when they are at their most fragile and vulnerable. Our most recent space, opened in August 2022, is in the Neonatal Intensive Care Unit at the John Hunter Children's Hospital. With the support of the Newcastle Permanent Charitable Foundation, we also established an equipment service that helps families to look after their child at home, in conjunction with hospital care. Through the Trust, we have also trained volunteers to support families with a child dealing with a life-limiting illness.

Making a difference to the lives of other children and their families has given Craig and me great satisfaction and has played a major role in our personal healing.

Watching our other sons grow and thrive as remarkable, compassionate and inspirational young men has also helped. Coming from a childhood shadowed by the uncertainty and distress of Nic's disease, they have risen to become successful in their respective professional fields and personal lives. Coen is a paediatrician/ infectious diseases specialist, and Alexander is a barrister in Sydney. We have two grandchildren who bring us great joy.

I haven't stopped running. When I run, I carry Nic's strength and light with every step. To date, I have run in 38 countries. Russia, Vietnam, Cuba and Portugal are particularly memorable, because in those countries, I've been lost. One wrong turn in an unknown place can add hours to a run. I also compete in marathons – New York, Boston, the Arctic Circle, Berlin, and the Gold Coast. I run for joy, to lose myself, to ponder the meaning of life, to build new friendships and, sometimes, to plan the rest of the day.

Nobody goes through life without being touched by the loss of someone they love, and there's nothing that can prepare you for the loss of a child. There are no consoling words I can offer to make the heartache stop, but there are many ways you can rebuild your life with your grief.

Allow your experience to propel you forward in achieving your goals and enriching your life. Life is not always fair, yet our response to injustice will heal the pain. Blame and grief can be crippling, but we can gain strength by giving back and helping to prevent others from travelling the same difficult road. We can't change circumstances, but we can use our sadness to find purpose, and through our empathy, we can give back to those who find themselves in a similar situation.

Focus on whatever you want to protect and build.

You will always feel a hollowness in your heart. The tears will never wash away the sadness, yet you are given but one chance to make a difference. The Nicholas Trust is inspired by Nicholas' courage. It is his legacy, and it is our belief that a journey of life deserves to end in dignity and peace.

It is so often that through adversity, we are challenged to make a difference. I am sometimes inspired by Margaret Mead, who said: 'Never doubt that a small group of thoughtful, committed citizens can change the world. Indeed, it is the only thing that ever has.'

Sometimes, simply turning up, being kind and spreading love is enough to make a difference to the people around you.

Never forget the fragility and preciousness of life and … and *seize the day!*

Chapter 8

The Power of Forgiveness

Grace Westworth

Rising from the loss of my son through surgery.

'The tragedy of losing my son is only a part of my life. It is not my whole life.'

Before the worst day of my life, my life was filled with the usual medley of ups and downs, happiness, sadness, laughter and tears. Like many women, I had experienced a marriage, the births and maturing of two sons, a divorce and a second marriage. My new husband and adult sons lived, worked and played together in Melbourne. I worked in a retirement village as an exercise instructor, which I thoroughly enjoyed.

Both of my sons, Leigh and Adam, were my rocks in hard times. When I had cancer, Leigh was particularly attentive and caring. He would have made a wonderful nurse. Leigh was also a creative, intelligent and funny young man who would impersonate friends and family and have us all in hysterics! With an inherited passion for cooking from my Maltese family, we enjoyed cooking together and playfully competing with our creations. With an entrepreneurial flare, Leigh had a bright future.

However, one of Leigh's main challenges in life was his fluctuating weight, which swung between normal and obese. This led to bullying at school and an increasing withdrawal from people. His self-esteem took a downward turn in his twenties when his retreat to his bedroom became more frequent and concerning. His significant weight gain and development of sleep apnoea during this time compounded our concern for his health and wellbeing.

In 2010, when Leigh was 27, he joined a new workplace and believed his position there would set him up with a solid and meaningful career. During his training, which he successfully completed, he lost a lot of weight that left him with excess skin around his abdomen. Months later, he called me in distress, telling me he was being bullied about his excess skin. He felt pressured to leave the workplace, which he soon did.

This was a huge disappointment to Leigh and our family. When he returned home, he was deeply depressed and unmotivated. Days spent in his room rolled into weeks, months and a couple of years. I felt helpless as I watched my son's mental and physical health decline.

Then, in 2013, the light in Leigh's spirit began to shine through. He decided to get his life back in order and, in doing so, he decided to have plastic surgery to remove his excess skin. He explained that the surgery would help him restore his self-esteem and mark the first step towards a better life. The family tried to convince him that he was a beautiful person just the way he was, but it was no use.

In 2014, lured by a medical tourism advertisement, Leigh went to a clinic in Kuala Lumpur, Malaysia, for a tummy tuck, liposuction, an upper eye lift, a chin tuck, lip filler, thigh lift and chest sculpting. We worried about him from the moment he told us.

Leigh underwent two major surgeries over five days. The first one lasted for 11 hours and the second one, just under five. A day after the second surgery, he was discharged from hospital and relocated to a hotel for ongoing wound treatment by visiting carers. The carers later reported finding Leigh in pain with the room 'in a mess with bloodstained robes, towels and bedsheets'.

In emails to me from his hotel, Leigh wrote about his pain, shortness of breath, rapid heartbeat, fainting spells and the neglect of the clinic. It was a frightening and distressing time for us all. Five weeks after the surgeries, Leigh was discharged and given permission to fly home, despite having gaping, leaking wounds and being in severe pain.

When I picked Leigh up from the Melbourne Airport on 11 May 2014, I was horrified by his condition. Slumped in his wheelchair, he wore dark sunglasses to hide his grief and pain, which he later told me was unbearable. Our plan was to take him to a medical clinic in Melbourne the next morning. However, within 24 hours, my son passed away in our home.

According to the coroner's report, the cause was a pulmonary thromboembolism, resulting from an undiagnosed blood clot. Had Leigh been tested and treated in a hospital with the appropriate technology, I believe he would be alive today.

For years, I tormented myself with guilt for not stopping Leigh from going to Malaysia. He was so determined, but if only I tried harder .... Each morning I would wake up, hoping it was just a nightmare, but then realise it was true. Leigh was gone forever.

A week after Leigh's passing, I returned to work feeling that it would be a good distraction, and I craved a sense of normality that a work routine provided. The residents at the village were kind, supportive and offered precious wisdom, which they earnt from many years of life experience. They made suggestions such as finding peace through religion and meditation.

The words of one woman particularly comforted me. 'Grace,' she said, 'you were a good mother and mentor to your son. Although you can't bring him back, Leigh will always be by your side. Accept the future and keep him close to your heart.'

Although often delivered in hidden tears, the fitness classes I gave were critical to my recovery. They gave me a reason to get out of bed each morning and boosted my physical and mental strength.

Due to the circumstances of Leigh's death, his funeral was a few weeks later. Journalists from newspapers, television and magazines hounded me for interviews. This was new and daunting to me, but I didn't want to let anyone down. Most importantly, I didn't want to let Leigh down. If Leigh's story could raise awareness of the impact of bullying or the danger of the medical tourism industry and prevent it happening to other people, I wanted to share it. I knew I had to be strong.

Eight years on, I have found peace.

Through stories and role-modelling, my father taught my family the importance of a strong mind *and* body. To care for our minds, we need to care for our bodies and vice versa. So, I exercised every day (fitness classes, walking and cycling), maintained good nutrition and practised a form of breathing therapy. My parents also exemplified the importance of maintaining an open, compassionate heart, despite what happened to you. I found these principles to be most helpful for my recovery.

I chose not to shy away from the world. I knew that Leigh would want me and our family to carry on and make the most of life. It also dawned on me that some people didn't know how to approach the subject of Leigh. So, I made them comfortable by letting them know that it was ok to ask or chat about Leigh, and that I liked them to speak openly about him. In fact, it still gives me pleasure hearing of other people's stories of Leigh and their times with him.

I also reached out for advice, especially from people who had experienced similar trauma. I joined a network of people who were dedicated to supporting bereaved parents

– Compassionate Friends. Although it's a network nobody wants to join, I found it helpful to talk to people who truly understood what I was going through.

If grief overwhelms me, I consciously change my thoughts to all the precious times I shared with my son, for these are my gifts, which I will treasure forever. I love telling stories to my grandchildren about their wonderful uncle. Whenever my grandchildren visit us, they light an incense stick and say a prayer to Leigh. When they ask me questions about him, my heart sings, as I know he will never be forgotten.

Nature was another healing agent. Living in a suburb doesn't mean isolation from nature. Every day, I'd look for her. Sometimes, I find her through my bedroom window as the sun rises, or in the autumn leaves that I walk upon, or in the birds that visit my verandah. Sometimes when I find her, I pray or meditate. There's something spiritual about nature that gives me strength and helps me to carry on.

I look at all the positives in my life – my other son, Adam, my husband, job, extended family and friends, which all give me reasons for purpose and gratitude.

Without the power of forgiveness, I wouldn't be who or where I am today. For my sake and the sake of those around me, I needed to forgive the people who bullied Leigh and forgive the medical team in Kuala Lumpur who failed in their duty to keep him safe and well. Forgiveness was not easy, but essential to my wellbeing.

So, how did I forgive?

Firstly, I *chose* to forgive through a conscious, heart-felt decision.

Secondly, I surrendered to the law of karma. Although I'm not a Buddhist, I believe that all actions, good and bad, are followed by consequences. Just as good actions produce good consequences, bad actions will lead to unhappiness. In Buddha's words: 'Not in the sky, nor in the middle of the ocean, nor in the cave of a mountain, nor anywhere else, is there a place, where one may escape from the consequences of an evil deed.'

Through the law of karma, there are consequences to those who let Leigh down, which I will never know. I just hope they learn from their actions and do not harm other people like they harmed my son. It's not my job to determine their consequences. My job is to be loving and happy for Leigh and everyone else around me.

The tragedy of losing my son is only a *part* of my life. It is not my whole life. Grief will always be a part of my emotional world, along with acceptance, joy, love, hope and the infinite tapestry of emotions that connect us all as humans.

To those who are suffering through grief, I say, release your guilt, anger and blame. By finding forgiveness in your heart, for yourself and others, you free yourself and *re-find* yourself, unshackled by the cage of toxicity.

My life has changed since the death of Leigh, and it will never be the same without him. It wasn't my choice to lose Leigh, but I do get to choose how to live without him. And I choose to smile, breathe, enjoy nature and those who are still around me.

Chapter 9

My Orange Angels

Kobe Steele, OAM

Rising from the loss of my daughter.

'You don't need to go to remote jungles to experience the wonder and awe of nature. Find "your Borneo", your green place that rejuvenates and inspires you.'

In my younger years, music was my life. When I was 18 years old, I landed my dream job – hosting my own national music television show, *Right On*, for Channel 10. Interviewing up-and-coming Australian rock bands and being paid to talk about my passion for music, I thought I was the luckiest woman alive!

If someone had walked into the studio then and told me that my future would be with orangutans, I would have laughed at them. Now, with the benefit of maturity, I can appreciate how the fickle finger of fate can dramatically change one's life.

Working and living in the belly of Australia's rock'n'roll world, falling in love with someone was inevitable. At the crazy young age of 20, I married Mark Evans, the bass player from AC/DC and, in 1982, our beautiful daughter Kristin was born. Our marriage eventually ran its course, and so Kristin became the centre of my world, my passion and my absolute reason for being.

As Kristin grew older and started school, rock'n'roll and school pick-ups didn't really go hand in hand, so I opened restaurants in Sydney's Palm Beach and then on the Gold Coast, Queensland, where I moved when Kristin was in her teens.

Kristin became a fantastic young woman. She was a complete individual, totally comfortable in her own skin, honest, intelligent, with an unparalleled 'joie de vivre'. I adored her, not just because she was my daughter, but for the person she had become. We laughed a lot and had so much fun together! Because I was young when I had her, we grew up together, and sometimes, Kristin was as much my mum, as I was hers.

After finishing university, Kristin set off to travel the world and while living in London she fell in love with a gorgeous Norwegian man, Chris. They were perfect for each other. They moved to Amsterdam and decided to get married. At the age of 25, Kristin was bursting with excitement about her impending wedding. I had never seen her so happy.

Then came the phone call. The call that nobody expects. The call that only happens to *other* people.

On a beautiful spring morning, Kristin was riding her bicycle to work. Only one block away from work, she was stopped at the red traffic lights at a major intersection. A wayward concrete truck illegally turned right against the red light, hit Kristin and took her life.

Imagine peering into a dark, bottomless well then tipping into it, tumbling down, down, darker, deeper, darker, never-ending despair. There is no way out, no way up. I locked my mind inside that well, and my body inside my house for the following three years. My tears never stopped, and I couldn't find a single reason to keep living. No matter how much time went by, I couldn't accept that she was gone … that I would never see her again, never hear her voice, never see her smile or hear her laugh. It simply couldn't be true!

What sustained me during those years was a combination of grief counselling and my *true* friends who stayed around to support me, along with my wonderful dad. In addition to the devastation of losing Kristin, I was bewildered and shocked by the number of 'friends' and family who vanished from my life after the accident. I grieved for them also.

Through counselling, I learnt that it isn't uncommon for people to disconnect from their grieving friends, because they find it too confronting. It makes them face their own fear of losing a loved one, so they walk away. Although this was incredibly painful at the time, I no longer take it personally ... though I still find it hard to fathom.

In their absence, however, I found the first-class quality of my remaining friends, whose kindness, patience and support I will never forget.

One such friend, Dr Stephen Van Mil, took me out for dinner and could tell I was a mess. 'I'm taking you to Borneo,' he said. 'The orangutans will help to heal you.' While I had always loved animals, this was the weirdest thing anyone had said to me! Besides, I was suffering from agoraphobia, and leaving my house for dinner was hard enough, let alone travelling into a Bornean jungle with a bunch of strangers. So, while I appreciated his good intentions, I declined his offer with a stack of excuses. But each time I created an excuse, my dear friend pushed back and refused to give up.

As my 50th birthday was drawing near, I finally agreed.

So, in late 2008, we arrived in Tanjung Puting National Park for an ecotour in Kalimantan, Borneo. It was the first time I had seen orangutans in the wild and, as you can imagine, I was absolutely in awe of these gentle, peaceful, sentient beings and felt so privileged to be in their rainforest home. Yet, while I was smiling on the outside (I became great at faking happiness), I still felt dead on the inside. My closed heart held so much pain, and I knew I would never feel happiness again.

That is, until I met someone who did.

After leaving the National Park, Stephen took me to a rehabilitation centre for orphaned and displaced orangutans, which was operated by Orangutan Foundation International (OFI). There, I met many orangutans in person and was lucky enough to visit the infant's playground where I spent time with a heap of little three- to five-year-old orangutans who had suffered the trauma of losing their mothers. They were the sweetest little bundles of love, play and affection. I even found myself smiling. Not a fake smile, but from a place of raw, authentic joy that I didn't think I could ever feel again.

Then I saw Faisal, a hairless three-year-old male who wasn't playing with the others. Instead, he sat in a corner by himself, looking shy and clearly deep in grief after losing his mother. My maternal instinct surged, and my sealed heart began to crack open. Little Faisal was eventually brave enough to leave the security of his corner, and he came over to me and gently climbed up into my arms. His gorgeous little face peered into my eyes and, through them, I believe he looked into my soul. He saw that I needed help, and I saw that he needed it too.

That was the moment. My heart burst open with lightning bolts of love and joy. Dear little Faisal gave me back my happiness!

On that magical day, I also met a female infant called Krista. She couldn't have been any cuter! She took me by the hand and dragged me around the forest, through the swamps, introducing me to her favourite trees. She was proudly showing me her home, like a human child would show a parent around a new kindergarten. All the way, she was giggling, tumbling, cheekily playing with her mates. The orangutans and I had the most wonderful couple of days, and I returned to Australia feeling like me again! I even cancelled my grief counselling!

I won't pretend it was all bubbles and bliss from then on. The tears continued, but much less frequently as my focus switched from my loss to what I needed to do to help orangutans. They had given me so much, and I wanted to do something for them. My newfound purpose gave me a reason to get out of bed, get out of my house and do something that was so much greater, and much more important than me.

Upon my return to Australia, not knowing what I could do to help, I researched ecotours to Borneo and discovered that just about everyone was profiting from the orangutans, except for the orangutans themselves. So, I began facilitating tours to Borneo as a means of raising funds for OFI.

In late 2012, while in Borneo with an ecotour group, I had the privilege of meeting OFI's founder, Dr Biruté Mary Galdikas. I was beside myself – like a school girl groupie in the presence of this absolute legend. Dr Galdikas is an internationally renowned environmentalist, anthropologist, and the world's foremost orangutan expert.

She explained to me that there was a remote piece of pristine rainforest that was up for sale. Elders who presided over the land had offered to sell this critical orangutan habitat to Dr Galdikas to preserve for the orangutans if she could raise the necessary funds. Otherwise, the land would be sold to the palm oil plantations who would decimate it. Dr Galdikas had fundraised tirelessly but had exhausted all channels and was $250,000 short. This was my chance to step up and help.

I returned home, founded the Orangutan Foundation International Australia, and with the help of friends and supporters, raised enough money to save the forest.

Orangutans share approximately 97 percent of our human DNA and 98 percent of our emotional intelligence. This means that in our fear, love, joy, grief, worry, frustration, excitement, humour, care, compassion and suffering – we are equal. And yet, this extraordinary, almost human mammal is in serious peril. Orangutans are classified as *critically* endangered – the reddest, loudest, highest risk of extinction. Can you imagine our world without the Faisals and Kristas? This is the stark reality unless we stop harming them and their rainforest habitat – and we can.

We all have a role to play in their survival, and there is no time for complacency. The rainforests of Borneo are the oldest in the world and are considered, along with the rainforests of the Amazon, the lungs of the Earth. Yet, driven by the high demand for palm oil, more than 80 percent have already been wiped out through deforestation. And keep in mind that deforestation is one of the greatest drivers of climate change.

To save orangutans, we must save the forests! One of the most effective ways to do this is by choosing products that are palm oil free. Unfortunately, many countries, including Australia, do not have mandatory oil labelling. The term 'vegetable oil' is often used in place of the words 'palm oil' to mask the name of the true ingredient. Many processed foods, beauty and cleaning products contain palm oil, but it's not hard to detect them. I encourage people to read the ingredients listed on products and avoid products that contain 'sodium laurel sulphate', 'glycerine' and 'vegetable oil', for a start. Our website (orangutanfoundation.org.au) offers more information. To save orangutans, we need a critical mass of conscious and compassionate consumers.

While I run a corporate merchandise company to pay my bills, OFI Australia is my 'love job'. It keeps me busy, engaged and energised. Whenever I return to Borneo, whether escorting ecotours or on other OFI business, I always catch up with Faisal and Krista and all my other little angels. Not that Faisal and Krista are little anymore! Faisal is now a large and handsome cheek-padded adult male. Krista is 15 or 16 years old and is always as happy to see me as I am her. She immediately climbs up on my back and insists on being piggy backed through the forest. Now weighing 35 kilograms, it takes every bit of my strength, but I love every second. Each time I go to Borneo, I return home feeling totally rejuvenated and strengthened in my resolve to protect them.

Over the years, I've been honoured with awards for my conservation work, including the Medal of the Order of Australia in the 2021. While I deeply appreciate the awards, my greatest reward comes from making a difference. This has been a critical key to my recovery from grief, but not my sole key. Support from my friends, attending counselling, practising gratitude and positive thinking have all contributed. While I still have negative thoughts, I don't give them much space, and I certainly don't let them overwhelm or consume me, like they used to.

Until recently, I thought I had had my 'fair share' of trauma, but of course life doesn't work that way. Trauma can strike any of us, at any time.

In May 2022, I was diagnosed with cancer. I cried for two weeks in hospital, but it wasn't a bottomless, giving up cry. It was a fear and dread of treatments cry on a foundation of hope. Once I accepted and adjusted to the situation, I applied most of the resilience tools that helped me rise from grief after losing Kristin: friends, gratitude, positive thinking, and my beloved orangutans.

This time, I was in control of the wheel, and I made sure I stayed on track. I'm presently through the other side of intense chemo and radiation treatment. While I am waiting for scans that will hopefully tell me I am now cancer free, I feel positive. My prognosis is good.

Out of every bad situation comes good, if your heart is open.

Kristin's death led me to orangutans, and therefore everything I do for them is Kristin's legacy. I know Kristin wouldn't want to see me depressed and crying. She would want to see me happy and thriving with purpose, living life to the full! I know that Kristin is holding my hand with each step of my journey, and I feel she is proud of me. That makes me happy.

My advice to those who are suffering in grief is to seek professional counselling as early as possible and avoid letting grief consume you permanently. Only surround yourself with positive people who have your best interests at heart. Please remember that there is no right or wrong way to grieve – and don't let anyone tell you differently. And most importantly, embrace the incredibly healing power of nature. You don't need to go to remote jungles to experience the wonder and awe of nature. Find 'your Borneo', your green place that rejuvenates and inspires you. If you open your heart in that green place, you might just find your purpose, your reason for getting up each day for the person you love. I did.

Chapter 10

The Most Beautiful Girl on Earth

Amina Abaza

Rising from childhood trauma and dealing with animal cruelty in Egypt.

'Once you find your way,
everything will be possible, as if God or the universe is waiting for you to take action.'

My life as a child in Cairo was seen by others as very pleasant – a good school, maids, a cook and driver. My parents looked cultured and refined, but behind the thin veil of privilege was an abused little girl. My father (a famous author) was big, tall and fat. With a loud voice and a violent demeanour, he was scary. Back then, it was common for parents to beat their children, and I remember being beaten for no reason.

One day, when I was four years old, a nun told my father that I was refusing to write, and even though it wasn't true, my father beat me savagely. The truth was that my mother forgot to put a pencil in my school bag, and so I didn't have anything to write *with*! This experience entrenched in me a heightened sensitivity to injustice and vulnerability.

Many similar events occurred over the years, and unfortunately, I found no sanctuary with either parent, as my mother would also beat me. There were no conversations between us. She would bark orders at me and leave me with maids who would sometimes have a turn at beating me too!

My saving angel was my grandmother, who treated me how children should be treated – with care, love and compassion. Ma knew that I was a smart and sensitive kid, ready to learn. She bought me books, taught me how to be a good person, to practise good manners, to never talk about the money I have, or show others that I was rich.

When I was eight, I experienced another pivotal life event. While waiting outside my house for a school bus, I befriended a stray white dog, who began waiting faithfully for me every day. I shared my school lunch with her and called her *La Plus Belle de la Terre*, which meant 'the most beautiful girl on Earth' in French.

Chapter 10

One night, I heard a gunshot outside my house and then an unforgettable howling of a dog. Sure enough, Plus Belle was shot. Like me, Plus Belle was vulnerable. Like me, she was a victim of injustice. From that moment, I was determined to help the most helpless in Egypt – the animals.

I grew up and became a successful career woman, holding the positions of chief translator for Egyptian Satellite Television and for the Minister of Animal Rights and Environment in the Women's Egyptian Government.

Yet, I never forgot Plus Belle.

In Egypt, neither the concept nor culture of animal welfare exists. In contrast, 5000 years ago, in ancient Pharaoh times, animals were revered, and Egypt was one of the most civilised countries in the world. Today, tragically, it's a very different place. The Egyptian Government controls the dog population with poison and guns. They often only wound the dogs, leaving them in the street to die in agony. Even children are drowning or burning puppies and kittens, as if it's a national pastime!

In 2001, inspired by Plus Belle, I established the first legitimate animal protection organisation in Egypt – the Society for the Protection of Animal Rights in Egypt (SPARE).

When you follow your passion, the universe supports you in the most unexpected ways. Through a rescued dog I was adopting, I met my husband, Raouf Mishriki.

I would get so depressed about the cruelty in Egypt, but Raouf told me to stop crying and get serious about stopping the atrocities. With sheer determination, we overcame a 'pyramid' of social and legal obstacles, and finally, SPARE became a registered charity, helping hundreds of dogs, cats, horses, donkeys and camels in Egypt.

Initially, I was ridiculed and criticised from all social levels for caring for animals before humans. But, when you're following your heart, you can cope with enormous pressures.

When you're following your heart, you're focused and immune to critics who want to derail you. In fact, my critics made me more determined to change the mindset that there is shame in defending animals. I would say to them, 'The ones who will not have mercy on the weak animal, will not have mercy on human beings.' We foster compassion towards *all* life.

While we have made a difference to the lives of many animals, we have a *long* way to go. Recently, another stray dog, Nagui, came into my life. A month before I met Nagui, he sniffed a piece of meat owned by a butcher in a slum area outside of Cairo. The outraged butcher retaliated by cutting off all his paws and dumping his tortured body on a street. Nagui miraculously survived for a month before someone brought him to me.

There have been many abused animals like Nagui who have end up on my doorstep. Many of whom have been well beyond saving, so I organised their euthanasia and stayed with them, comforting them as they gently passed. However, there was something special about Nagui. Perhaps it was his intelligence, his nobleness, or his 'I see all' eyes that struck me. Whatever it was, I told him that I would do whatever it took to save him. I thought that, with advancements in prosthetics, he could have a good life without paws. Sadly, however, as the sun rose one morning, his gentle heart stopped beating. While we couldn't save his life, my team and I surrounded him with love as he passed.

This tragedy really tested my resilience. I cried for many

hours and am still grieving while I write this. To console myself, I choose to believe that Nagui stayed alive to find me, not for a longer life, but to experience kindness for the first time in his life. May his gentle soul rest in peace.

Sometimes, I say to myself, 'I've seen it all now. There is not an act of torture, neglect or abuse to animals that would shock me'. Then, nope – I'm wrong again! Time and time again, I witness different mutilations, different ways people make money or entertain themselves through deliberate acts of violence against animals.

While many acts of cruelty are transparent, others are more covert and devious. Pet shops, for example, are filled with beautiful, *stolen* dogs that are caged in dark basements – the dogs are hungry, frightened, confused and calling desperately for help to ears that don't hear them.

Animal welfare charities in my country are not regulated and therefore attract corrupt people who capture and steal animals off the streets, setting themselves up as a charity and taking money from sympathetic international donors. Instead of using the funds to help the (stolen) animals, they buy cars, homes and the like for themselves. They exploit both the animals and the donors, and they murk the reputation of the legitimate organisations.

Consequently, I disassociate with other organisations in Egypt by funding SPARE myself. I neither ask for or accept donations. Speaking out about the rife corruption in animal welfare charities comes at a cost. I've been slandered, abused and threatened by the perpetrators, but how can I be silent while the suffering and injustice continues?

As Edmund Burke famously said, 'The only thing necessary for the triumph of evil is for good men to do nothing.'

It is my dream to make a documentary about the devolution of the treatment of animals in Egypt. In Mahatma Gandhi's words, 'The greatness of a nation and its moral progress can be judged by the way its animals are treated.' In making this documentary, I want to remind my brothers and sisters where we've come from, and how we can return to a compassionate and civilised society. It is this goal, rooted in the core of my heart and soul, that motivates me to recover from my own trauma, keep going and succeed.

I am privileged to live in a magnificent home, surrounded by the animals who have found sanctuary at SPARE. They give me satisfaction and joy every day. Although my soulmate Raouf passed away in 2021, I have friends and family far flung around the world who give me strength when I'm weak. Their support is appreciated and never forgotten, for we cannot get through life, or make changes alone.

If it was not for the suffering I endured as a child, I wouldn't have the empathy, sympathy, determination and strength to be who I am today. I have no doubt that the resilience I fostered as a child prepared me for the challenges I faced when establishing SPARE and continue to face today.

I found my inner peace and happiness when I found my purpose, my 'way'. When you are in hard times, dig deep for your inner strength. It will be there when you need it. Draw your own life and use courage to not let other people draw it for you. Once you find your way, everything will be possible, as if God or the universe is waiting for you to take action. When you follow your heart, the universe *will* work for you.

Chapter 11

Bitten and Stung, but Not Shy

Vicki Simlesa

Rising from a life-changing injury.

'When you experience a close call to death, your values and beliefs are scrambled and re-ordered.'

Animals and sport were always the main features of my life, including when I grew up with a big, loving family on the Sunshine Coast, Queensland. When my sister moved to the Northern Territory, I fell in love with its rugged, magnificent, unspoilt environment and relaxed culture after one visit.

I then moved to Darwin in 1983 and thrived in a sporting and outdoor lifestyle, playing touch football, women's rugby and basketball. I was in the first national Northern Territory women's rugby team and competed in Canberra.

Equal to my love of sport is my love of nature, so I also embraced orienteering, hiking, fishing, camping and gardening.

In 1985, when I applied for a job with the Northern Territory Government as a trainee in the veterinary laboratories, I imagined I'd be with fluffy rabbits and test tubes. Instead, I was delegated the animals that nobody really wanted, the ones that could sting, kick and bite!

Initially, I worked in the field with large animals such as cattle and buffalo, while completing a Diploma of Applied Science. Knowing that I was contributing to environmental conservation, it was my dream job.

Not only did I love the meaningful work, I found great joy in the ability it gave me to travel the world annually during my holidays. I have travelled to Asia, Africa, Europe, and the Americas, learning much about the various countries, cultures, and human behaviours. Most importantly, I learnt that Australia really is a lucky country, and life here is far easier and freer than many other countries. I'd always return from my trips with a renewed appreciation of home.

In 1993, I was offered a job as a crocodile technician,

researching crocodiles on farms across the Top End of Australia. The purpose of the research was to develop the best practice in crocodile husbandry. For a moment, I paused and thought, *that sounds dangerous. But it could also be exciting!*

For the first month or so, I found the crocodiles both terrifying and fascinating.

A crocodile's jaw has the strongest bite in the animal kingdom, about ten times more powerful than the great white shark. And they can even close a valve in their heart to allow them to submerge underwater for up to an hour. One more fact for your next trivia game is that crocodiles have the most acidic stomach of any vertebrate, which allows them to dissolve and digest bones, hooves and horns from their prey. They really are amazing animals that deserve our respect.

Most of my work was conducted on crocodile farms, where I learnt about handling crocodiles and their behaviours. Once I overcame my fear, I handled crocs like a seasoned stockwoman would handle cattle. Like any seasoned stockperson, however, we learn from hard lessons. If the crocodile is not offered enough respect, it is extremely dangerous, as I found out.

In 1996, while working on a farm in the Katherine region, I was routinely auditing the crocodiles and entered the pens to gain accurate numbers. An adult crocodile swung his head around and bit my right leg. I was lucky that it was only a warning. If it had been an intentional attack, I wouldn't be here to talk about it.

Although the bite wounds were not concerning, the infection from the crocodile's teeth that soon followed was alarming. The infection quickly spread throughout my body and confined me to hospital for over four weeks. Sore and unable to move for the first week, my mobility slowly returned. As you can imagine, I was the talk of the town for a while! Crocodile victims make the news.

I gained a valuable lesson from this, which was to not be complacent around animals of strength and power. I learnt to be more alert and a hell of a lot more respectful.

In early 2003, the deadly varroa mite was discovered in New Zealand. The mite, which acts as a parasite in beehives, can quickly destroy bee populations. Australia, therefore, established a national program for early detection of disease and pests that harm bees. The NT adopted the program and, as a new Apiary Officer, I became the 'bee lady of the NT'.

Again, I loved this role and became fascinated with bees as much as crocodiles. The job of a beekeeper in the Northern Territory, however, is not for the frail – picture yourself wearing a bee suit in the high humidity of a sunny 30-degree Celsius day! No diet program in the world could produce the same results of weight lost as one day in a bee suit in the NT!

Bees, like crocodiles, are amazing animals and can be just as dangerous. If you are afraid or nervous around them, you will get stung. I have been stung too many times to count, but as a beekeeper, getting stung is commonplace. However, no matter how many times you get stung, every sting hurts. You just accept it.

I prefer bees over people. I can trust bees. I know when they are upset and when they are going to sting me. Pretty much any animal is predictable, but humans can't be predicted.

With more than 20 years' experience working for environmental conservation in a part of Australia I loved, in balance with sport and travelling, my life was great.

However, in 2009, it suddenly changed.

My partner at the time had pet snakes, and we kept rats as a food source. I would dutifully clean and feed the rats, as one does! One day, while cleaning the rats' cage, I was bitten on the finger. I cleaned and treated the wound and didn't think much more of it. About a week later, I became sick. Not a 'Panadol and rest in bed' sick, but a 'scary, never felt before, help me' sick. The sore joints came first, followed by extreme thirst and nausea.

I took myself to hospital and was told it was food poisoning. 'Go home. You'll be better soon,' they said. I followed their advice and returned home. However, I constantly felt thirsty, and I eventually stopped urinating and could barely walk. My partner took me to a doctor and upon arriving at the clinic, I was immediately transferred by ambulance to hospital.

From here, everything went to hell.

The emergency department determined I had a chronic infection that shut down my kidneys and liver and it was shutting down my heart and leaving me completely disabled. The doctors said they had no idea what was happening and that unless they could figure it out, I had 48 hours to live.

They tubed me with Penicillin, suggested that I take care of my affairs and say goodbye to my family.

My whole world then imploded. To be told that you are going to die and can't do anything about it is crippling. I just sat in my hospital bed in shock. My sister was on her way to me, but then and there, I was alone and had no idea what to say to my family when they eventually came, if they came in time.

The pain in my joints was extreme, and the doctors doped me up to sleep for a while. Therefore, the next couple of days were foggy. I do, however, remember waking up to be told that the Penicillin was curing the mystery infection. My kidneys and liver also began to reactivate, and my heart had not sustained any damage. Unfortunately, my joints were a different matter.

I suffered 'elephantiasis-like' symptoms where my joints swelled so much that my joint capsule in both ankles ruptured. My left shoulder fell out of its socket, and both of my knees swelled to four times their normal size.

It took a week, and telling my rat bite story, before I was diagnosed with Rat Bite Fever – a rare disease that, even more rarely, can cause the full-blown symptoms that I experienced.

At that stage, I was still unable to walk due to my painful, swollen joints. A consequence of the disease is permanent rheumatoid arthritis. However, I was alive, and my view of life had irreversibly changed. Being told that you are going to die gives you an appreciation for life that you otherwise wouldn't have. In that sense, being told that I was going to die was a gift.

When you experience a close call to death, your values and beliefs are scrambled and re-ordered. Issues such as money and future security are no longer so important. Don't get me wrong, preparing for the future is important, but I no longer worry about it. I'm more focused on the present – my tasks and activities at hand. A new appreciation for life was born within me, and with that came an acceptance of what I couldn't change. If I couldn't change it, why worry about it?

Four months later, I was released from hospital in a wheelchair. I started to walk again in short distances and couldn't stand for long periods. However, day by day, I slowly improved physically – mentally was a different challenge.

In hospital, my thoughts were largely positive, focusing on recovering and getting home. Once that was achieved, the reality that my life had now changed completely sunk in. My outdoor activities of orienteering and hiking were over forever. Running, playing contact sports and endurance activities were no longer possible. Facing this reality was the hardest part of all my challenges.

My sport and outdoor activities were my tonic and nourishment. The tap was now turned off, and I consequently suffered a period of depression. Doctors gave me anti-depression medication, which helped for a while, but for me, it was not a long-term solution. I needed to find new sources of tonic and nourishment and turn the tap back on.

I accepted my new limitations and adapted to change. Instead of tormenting myself with thoughts about what I *wish* I could do, I focused on things that I still *could* do: fishing, camping, and short walks with my dogs. Gardening and taking care of my chickens and dogs on my rural block now occupies my time after work and still allows me that connection with the outdoors that I crave.

It took time, self-discipline and patience to be satisfied with my current lifestyle. It is still hard sometimes. I miss the comradery, fitness and friendships that came with my old sports and activities, but I have accepted my reality and am at peace.

However, my health challenges are far from over.

Within the next ten to 15 years, I will need to have both my ankles replaced, so I can continue to walk. Rather than worry, I use self-discipline to stay in the present.

Sometimes, I wish I could go back in time and replay things differently, but such thoughts don't help me. So, I replace them with more helpful thoughts, such as gratitude for everything that's going well. Afterall, I have a meaningful job that I love. I have a home in the bush, great friends, my husband, children, dogs, and a loving family.

I have faced death at least once, maybe twice, and am gratefully still alive. No matter what life throws at you, don't get stuck in a hard place. Keeping moving. If you keep moving forward, learn to accept what you can't change, and do things that calm you and make you feel good, then life will get a little easier each day.

My late father once said to me, and it has always stuck, 'You are who you are, and other people's approval is not needed. Be honest with yourself.'

The most important lesson that I have learnt out of all of this, is that tomorrow may never come. Remember the past, it was who you were. Plan for the future, but live for today.

Photo by Terry Scott

Chapter 12

The Strength of Our Dreams

Kate Steels

Rising from the loss of my son.

'Only through tragedy do you really understand the fragility of life, which is so very precious.'

They say that losing your child is the most distressing experience that life can dish out to you. Losing a child through death by suicide adds another layer of complexity. I've been there, in that dark cave of shock, denial, depression, anger, guilt, blame, confusion and despair. And I kept walking through that cave.

Sometimes I fell over and wept, but I pulled myself up again, often with help from others, and I kept walking until I looked up and saw a pinpoint of light. As I walked towards the light, it opened. It was so large that fresh air from the other side brushed my face. I inhaled the air and climbed through to the other side. Out of the cave, I stretched and looked at the great horizon ahead of me. I found the light in my cave and share my story in hope that it helps you to find the light in yours.

I grew up in a loving family in England and went to Durham University. I married and, in 1999, gave birth to my gorgeous son, Daniel. My blissful family life, however, was short-lived. In 2008, my marriage came to an abrupt and traumatic end. I clawed my way through a tumultuous divorce and ended up as a single mother to Daniel. I did my best juggling work and motherhood and, together with our pet rabbit and rescued hedgehog, we created a new home.

Our happiest times were crowned by our travelling adventures. With our shared love of skiing and scuba-diving, we travelled to some exotic parts of the world, including Egypt, Australia, and Europe. Daniel was close to my parents and extended family, with whom we spent many wonderful holidays.

Despite my efforts to adjust to my new single lifestyle,

I felt a deep emptiness and loneliness on the weekends and evenings when Daniel was with his father. To fill this void, I turned to my childhood love of sport. I began building my fitness with gym exercises and swimming in a local pool. While my fitness was building, so was my confidence and openness to new possibilities. It was during this transformative period that two of my childhood dreams resurfaced – to swim the English Channel solo, and to also go to Antarctica.

In 2009, I joined a local triathlon club and swam in the sea at the Southsea Beach, Portsmouth. It was there I discovered that open water is 'my space' where I can feel at ease and find my reset button. My open-water swimming journey was born.

In 2011, I swam the English Channel as part of a relay team. It was an exciting achievement, which affirmed to me that swimming the Channel *solo* is possible. After five years of regular training, I was able to 'tick off' that goal. The experience felt surreal, yet at the same time, I was quietly proud. Afterwards, I realised that this wouldn't be my only swimming goal, and I opened myself to a world of possibilities.

By this stage, I was swimming through the winter and enjoying both the challenge and exhilaration that often accompanied cold-water swimming, so I decided to stretch myself further by swimming in icy water. This meant swimming in water five degrees Celsius or less, wearing just bathers, a cap and goggles. I soon found myself thriving in this extreme sport, both mentally and physically.

Although Daniel couldn't understand my attraction to ice-water swimming, especially as he witnessed how cold I would get, he was proud of my achievements. One chilly

Christmas, he was even persuaded to have an icy dip in a local river with me, following a bet with my brother!

In 2018, just two days after Daniel started university, my beloved son took his own life, totally unexpectedly. I can't put into words the pain and grief of losing your only child.

In my experience, many people don't know how to handle this situation. Some don't know which words to use, so they simply go quiet, or completely disappear from the radar! Perhaps they're frightened that it could happen to someone in their family, or that they could somehow be linked to the tragedy. I don't know why, but losing a child through suicide certainly sifts out your true friends, who stay and support you.

After Daniel died, I experienced a plethora of emotions – from anger at him for leaving us, anger that he didn't call me or trust me or anyone else to help him, to sorrow from imagining what he was feeling, and from the immense guilt and frustration of not understanding why such a bright 19-year-old would think that suicide was his best or only solution.

Some people, albeit with good intentions, say or imply that you will 'get over it' or 'move on'. However, you can never 'get over' the loss of a child, but you can certainly learn to live with the loss and make room in your life for peace, love and joy.

Four years later and not a single day has passed without thinking about and missing Daniel. Occasionally, I sink into lows. Sometimes, I can anticipate them – around birthdays, Christmas and Easter – but other times are triggered unexpectedly. It could be a place we had been together, or when seeing other young men around the same age, or when

I hear or see something that would have made Daniel laugh. Such triggers are sufficient to open the wounds.

When I lost my marriage and later faced other problems, I thought of less fortunate people than myself. In Pakistan, for example, floods were washing away family members and homes. I remember donating to disaster appeals and being grateful that while times were tough for me, I still had Daniel and a roof over our heads. This coping mechanism, however, no longer worked for me. Daniel was gone and, granted I had bricks and mortar, it didn't feel like home anymore.

So, what kept me going through this time? Primarily, it was my family. I *needed* to rise again for their sake. My family was my 'why'.

My family, partner and *true* friends were my 'how'. Through their constant support, I found inner strength to get through the abyss, one day at a time.

Shortly after Daniel's passing, I was introduced to another source of support – a group called Survivors of those Bereaved by Suicide (SOBS). The volunteers who run the group are amazing and have lived the experience. The group sessions were painful but enormously helpful. People from all walks of life were pulled together by a common tragedy and shared their feelings and experiences with others who trusted and understood them.

Of equal importance in my healing journey was my open-water and ice swimming. Daniel was always supportive of his quirky mother who loved swimming. I continue swimming now partly in his memory and partly for my own wellbeing. The water is my happy place, where I can refocus and wash away my sadness and stress. Although each open-water experience is different – the weather, the waves, the wildlife, the company I have before, during and afterwards – they all have one thing in common: when I immerse myself in water, I transform.

I am blessed to have a big circle of international swimming friends, particularly through my ice-swimming network. Since Daniel died, I have been given extraordinary opportunities, which, although daunting at first, I embraced. Ram Barkai, founder, president and CEO of the International Ice Swimming Association, invited me to become the secretary to the global board – a hugely prestigious role, for which I am honoured. A year later, I was honoured again by my induction into the International Ice Swimming Hall of Fame.

Ice swimming and travel became an integral part of my life. I enjoyed competing and making friends around the world.

There is an 'adventurous' side to ice swimming, which is about individual ice mile challenges – where one swims 1609 metres in water *below* five degrees Celsius.

The ultimate global challenge is the Ice Seven. This comprises of completing in an ice mile in each continent of the world, with no wetsuit, gloves or booties, only bathers, goggles and a swimming cap. Over six years, I pursued the Ice Seven in the United Kingdom, Norway, Morocco, China, Canada, New Zealand, and finally in Argentina.

The Ice Seven has a catch. One of the ice miles must be swum at zero degrees. On Christmas Eve in 2017, I did mine in China. It was the toughest swim of my life, with a wind chill of minus 22 degrees Celsius. With sheer grit and determination to complete this mile, I was pushed to my limit. I had to trust my support team 100 percent, who were constantly watching and monitoring me.

I also wouldn't have been able to do it without my good Russian friend who is an expert in rewarming very cold people by using a special method. Initially, my hands and feet go in buckets of cold water, which at first feel warm. Hot towels are then wrapped around my kidneys, groin and neck. It's important to rewarm carefully because if cold blood rushes from your extremities to your core, it can cause you to collapse or experience a heart attack, or even die. Once I start to rewarm, I move into a sauna for the final part.

After my swims, I am always exhausted but elated.

At the end of 2020, I was diagnosed with a brain aneurysm. I knew nothing about aneurysms at the time but was fortunate to have access to excellent international specialists who understood the effects of ice swimming on the body. The size of my aneurysm was borderline in the United Kingdom. I had a choice whether to have surgery, or not. Without surgery, I couldn't swim again in cold water.

For a while, I contemplated returning to trekking as my new main sport, for I loved my expeditions in Papua New Guinea as a teenager, and later in the Himalayas. However, I was advised not to go to places of remoteness or high altitude, as there was a substantial risk that I could suffer from a brain injury or even die.

How could I possibly cope without Daniel and without a sport, I asked myself.

The possibility was unimaginable.

In January 2021, I therefore had brain surgery. Unfortunately, it was during the peak of the UK COVID crisis, but both the operation and recovery went well. With gym exercises and ice baths, my fitness and pursuit of the Ice Seven were restored.

My final Ice Seven swim was in the stunning Lake Esmeralda, in Argentina, in November 2021. This swim was different. I swam in memory of Daniel and for everyone else who reaches a point where they *feel* there is no way out (even though there always is). The event raised funds for and awareness of the Samaritans, a UK not-for-profit organisation that saves lives through suicide prevention.

With only three people in the world to ever achieve the Ice Seven, it marked the pinnacle of my swimming career. From here, at the age of 52, I thought it was time to 'give back'. Afterall, I couldn't have achieved my success without the support of many other people.

After obtaining an open-water coaching qualification, I began coaching others in this wonderful sport. I am particularly proud of a team of six teenage girls who successfully swam a relay across the English Channel and won three awards.

In 2022, I was honoured to become the World Open Water Woman Swimmer of the Year 2021. I never dreamt I would ever be shortlisted, let alone win. I am profoundly grateful to everyone who voted for me, believed in me and supported me over the years.

The year 2022 has been an exceptional year, not only due to the accolades I've been honoured to receive, but also because I learnt to enjoy myself despite not having Daniel in my life. I gave myself permission to be happy. In my heart, I know that Daniel would have wanted me to keep living, swimming, and enjoying myself, so I do.

In the summer of 2022, I swam 40 kilometres down the river Danube in Romania, the Catalina Channel, and around Jersey in the United Kingdom. My partner also joined me for an Alcatraz swim in San Francisco.

Since Daniel took his life, my appreciation for life has magnified. Only through tragedy do you really understand the fragility of life, which is so very precious. As I cherish the many wonderful memories I have of Daniel, I'm inspired to make more great memories. Our life, after all, is a bank of memories.

Balance in my work and life is now supremely important to me. I have a wonderful job with a team and an employer who understand my need to swim. I am thankful for their empathy and flexibility.

Self-care and authenticity are other factors that have contributed to my wellbeing. Nature and water are my tonics, which I take as often as possible, in balance with my work. Challenges, adventure and travel make me 'tick'. They make me … me! And by being authentically me, I attract like-minded people and thrive in my tribe.

Please don't misunderstand. It's not sunshine and rainbows every day. In fact, I still dread Christmas. I dread the long crescendo of Christmas that starts way too early – the carols in supermarkets, the office parties, the decorations. Each reminder of Christmas is a stick that pokes my heart – *ha, ha, it's family time, and you don't have Daniel!* However, I'm well aware that such tormenting thoughts don't help me, and I am committed to replacing them.

Since losing Daniel, I have spent much time pondering suicide prevention, particularly for teenagers. The effect of suicide and the ripple effect on others is immense. In the United Kingdom, 16 people take their own lives each day.

While technology and the internet have benefits, they also have a dark side and exacerbate pressure on teenagers.

Pressure to have expensive technology, to be 'tapped on' to the internet for social media, or perhaps gaming. Many teenagers prefer to stay inside, online, rather than being outside with friends or nature. They are disconnected from these vital life forces. Teenagers are our future, and their relationship with technology is a major social problem that warrants urgent attention.

Mainstream education systems also increase pressure on teenagers. With a constant bombardment of academic tests and examinations, critical areas of life – such as relationships and character-building (including resilience and empathy) – barely get a 'look in'. More focus needs to be given to prepare teenagers for life beyond school, including where and how to get support if they are in a crisis. I urge all parents, carers and teachers of youngsters to engage with them and empower them with resilience skills. This would have helped Daniel and might have saved his life.

My advice to those young and old, who may be struggling in that dark cave where I've been, is that I promise you there is light. Equip yourself with whatever tools you need to find it, and you will.

Talk. Open yourself to a friend, a family member, or someone anonymous in a charity. With help from others, you *will* get through your ordeal.

Go outside. Get fresh air and enjoy nature. I don't mean for Instagram shots, I mean *earnestly* connect with nature.

Move your body through exercise or sport. You don't have to be good at it. Think about learning something new, perhaps with a friend! Research has shown that exercise is one of the best things we can do for our wellbeing.

Social media is not a balanced or accurate reflection of

real life. Understand that *everyone* struggles sometimes and recovers. And we may struggle again and again, but we keep rising and learning and strengthening each time.

You are never alone in that cave. Ask for help, and the light will soon shine for you too.

Chapter 13

Sailing through Storms

Jacqueline Hope

Rising from a broken heart and dealing with disease.

'Recognise suffering as a sign of respect for that which you had the privilege to enjoy before it changed.'

A life without hardships is an unrealistic expectation. It's just that some trials are bigger than others. In recent years, I have experienced three quite different challenges.

I am not a brave person as such. I have completely irrational fears of snakes and heights. I'm sometimes afraid of the dark, of crowds, of public speaking, of failure. The list goes on.

For the most part, it is fear of the unknown, of something in the future, which may or may not happen, something that has captured my imagination so vividly that it seems as if real.

I have also known the more visceral fear of the immediate threat to my life, but that usually passes more quickly, subsiding after the rapid adrenaline spike.

I don't consider my solo circumnavigation of the world a hardship. It was, after all, a challenge that I chose. My life before then, however, was quite different.

Partnered with a fellow sailor, a perfect match by all accounts, and living aboard a 56-foot yacht in Queensland, I enjoyed the camaraderie of the sailing community around us. In winter, we would either sail off to the warmth of the South Pacific Islands or fly to our smaller (46-foot) yacht to cruise the Mediterranean. It was certainly an enviable lifestyle, with early retirement investments making it possible for me to not have to work, while my partner still worked remotely.

But I have jumped two steps back, to the idealised contrast, if you like, to my 'earlier comfort zone'. Yes, I was about as comfortable as it was humanly possible to be.

Then came the fall from grace, which I never saw coming,

so it hit all the harder.

After my partner's mother died, leaving him a princely inheritance, my beloved soulmate sailed off with his best friend's wife. Naturally, I berated myself endlessly with my innumerable and unforgiveable shortcomings, which didn't help at all. If only I had done this differently, or that differently, or been a different person altogether, one more to his liking, then he wouldn't have strayed.

So, gathering up what few possessions I had, and the shattered pieces of my tattered pride, I returned to my family in Melbourne. While my wonderful adult children and beautiful grandchildren were loving and supportive, I felt an enormous void for the soulmate that I believed I would share the rest of my life with. And the resources that I once would have had to help me cope with such loss – my glorious lifestyle, the yachts, the community I had cultivated – had all but vanished.

I think I then slumped quite deeply through the recognised stages of loss – disbelief, denial, anger, grief, self-recrimination, depression. I really thought my sailing days were done, and I couldn't bear to even look at a boat without bursting into tears. Old friends with good intentions rallied, offering to take me out sailing with them, which only made things worse.

I would like to say that my own resilience tools pulled me out of it, and of course I did make use of all the tricks of old, plus a few new ones, which no doubt helped a bit.

Whenever I found myself obsessing over the 'could have's' and 'should have's', I would give myself a little pinch on the arm and say to myself, 'stop it!', and the distraction of a more physical pain helped shift the emotional one.

Another strategy I developed as I lay awake in the middle of the night was to metaphorically wrap my thoughts up in a bundle, and then envisage myself placing them into a drawstring bag in the corner of the room and telling myself I would deal with them in the morning. Naturally, they wriggled and squirmed like a bag of snakes.

Then there was something I called the 'watched pot'.

To still my runaway thoughts, I would say to myself, 'Ok, you can have free reign for the next ten minutes; go for it; do your darndest. If you want to pick the scabs off the wounds until they bleed, go right ahead.' Strangely enough, the mental maelstrom doesn't like to be so coldly observed. It's rather like asking the question, 'I wonder what my next thought will be?' and watching intently for it.

To only find … a blank ….

Other resilience tools included making as much effort as I could to eat well and exercise regularly. I must have walked a thousand miles, often alarming others when my grumbling thoughts spilled over into outer earshot. I tried to avoid binging on food, alcohol, drugs, Netflix, or other escapist, mind-numbing blankets, though this proved not always successful. I understood it was important to be kind to myself, to give myself time and allow myself to fall through the odd crack, to forgive my weaknesses.

Then there were the tried-and-true philosophical adages that aim to put things into more positive perspectives, such as, 'whatever doesn't kill you makes you stronger' and 'there's a positive side to this' and 'there's a lesson here that you need to learn' and 'one door closes and another opens' … and best of all, 'this too shall pass'. And ultimately, it did pass.

About a year later, something inside of me woke up

stronger, and I saw my loss as my gain. Here was an opportunity for me! I was single, still relatively fit and able. Having wanted to sail around the world alone since I was a young child, I considered that perhaps now was the time to resurrect that dream … alone.

So, I set about preparing for that mission in earnest, ready to take on the ocean, which seemed a more reasonable foe, perhaps more impersonal at least, less reactive to my personal shortcomings. It could knock me down in a fair fight.

It seems to me that there are different kinds of challenges in life. Some just knock us right over, and no amount of ducking and weaving and clever mind-speak can change it or alter the pain we are going through. These are the ones that are not of our choosing, such as getting cancer.

The challenges I experienced sailing around the world alone were of a different ilk, perhaps because this was something I had *chosen* to do. It was the fulfilment of my childhood dream. Of course, Mother Nature threw a lot of things at me over which I had no control. Again, it was up to me to choose how to respond to those. It's true, sometimes we find ourselves in the mud, and the more we kick and flail and splash about, the more we spread the mud.

One night while sailing, it was pitch black (these things like to happen at night) and I could smell the storm building quietly like a malevolent force on the horizon. All was eerily still.

It's the waiting, the imminent pounding, the strength of which you can never know in advance, and the dread of the unknown that rattles your teeth.

I was on high alert, like a dog with its hackles up, sniffing danger. It wasn't the first storm I'd been through, nor was it the last. Each one of them is different, and each adds a notch to my confidence quota.

But there's always the doubt, the worry, the fear. *Will this one be stronger, wilder, more life-threatening? Will it catch me out in a moment unawares? Will it hit from a different angle that the boat can't endure? Are the boat and I being slowly worn down in unseen ways that will eventually crack open?*

Like a coiled snake the storm finally struck.

Shanti was thrust hard over on her side and white water flooded the cockpit. My heart pounded as I struggled to regain control. Yes. Control was the thing.

Fear can so easily cripple us when we feel out of control. In that moment between panic and action, the external fact of the storm was less threatening than my emotional response to it. My survival was in my mind more than my hands.

And when the storm passed, I was left with a sense of elation at having braved it. As wind and waves abated and the sun restored peace, I felt fully alive, so much a part of everything that I gave thanks from the bottom of my heart.

In some ways, the suffering and the release are intertwined, like night and day.

It's ok to suffer, to feel fear, to lose control, to regain it, to grow from the experience. I am learning to 'allow' and have a deep acceptance of 'what is'.

Being diagnosed with a rare type of leukemia then pushed me deeper into the realm of acceptance.

Again, this is a different kind of hardship, somewhere in between a storm at sea and a broken heart. Storms are generally quite short-lived, much shorter than broken hearts. A potentially fatal illness is a whole different ballgame.

For the best part of a year, I handed my body over to

the medical system, placing my trust in strangers to pull me through this dark tunnel. It went against everything I had previously believed in, having been a natural health practitioner, always taking responsibility for my own health.

But when those alarms bellowed in the middle of the night, and the room filled with anxious-looking doctors who pumped chemicals into my veins, I could only hope they got it right. When the gurney I was lifted onto hurtled down narrow corridors of the deep bowels of the hospital, I marvelled that there were people working those graveyard shifts, ready to receive my body and do it whatever was required.

Filled with gratitude, I let go of all my tightly held preconceptions. They were of no use to me in this unfamiliar territory. At that point, I felt a certain detachment from my body, recognising that my body was not me.

A smile curved my lips as the thought came that it would be tacky of me to die after they had gone to so much trouble to keep this body alive.

So, I dug deeper.

When it seems like we have nothing left inside, as if we are scraped out like a deboned chicken, somehow, we pull (or are pulled) through. It really is quite a miraculous thing, the resilience of the human spirit.

Life becomes so much more precious when it has been threatened. Having so often faced the possibility of death, my predominant feeling now is of gratitude. Each sunrise adds another day to my first year in remission, and it gives me a renewed appreciation of the small things, which are so huge.

There are no traffic lights on my island home. Curlews masquerade as garden ornaments and kookaburras cackle in the naked gums. The slower pace permits a smile or greeting. I have time to sing, walk, notice the birds, the sky, the trees, and reconnect with the things I love.

Storms of various kinds are bound to upset our lives. Accept them as you would the night, knowing that day will surely follow. Recognise suffering as a sign of respect for that which you had the privilege to enjoy before it changed. Know that change is inevitable. Make a practice of imagining the future as it will be, after the hardship has passed.

Chapter 14

Leaving a Light On

Suzie Ratcliffe

Rising from the loss of my kidnapped sister.

'Given all that Mum had lost, her resilience continues to motivate me to be my best version of me.'

'Go Redlegs!' was my family's catchcry before I was born. My family were avid football supporters of the Norwood Football Club in South Australia and watched their team as often as possible. The game on 25 August 1973 was like any other at the Adelaide Oval. Mum, Dad, my brother David, who was 13, and my sister Joanne, who was 11, were all there. Joining them that day was Rita, a football acquaintance of our parents, and her four-year-old granddaughter Kirste.

Joanne was a caring and motherly type of girl and instantly took Kirste under her wing, keeping her occupied while the game was playing. During the game, Kirste required the toilet, and Joanne offered to take her. The toilets were located just beneath the grandstand in a 'runway' where Joanne had often been. The girls returned soon after.

Near the end of the third quarter, Kirste required the toilet again, and Joanne escorted her again.

Our family rule was to never go to the toilet or wander around during breaks in the game or during the final quarter when the grounds became extra busy. Joanne knew this rule and would have ensured they returned quickly. However, 15 minutes after the girls had left, they hadn't come back, and my parents became concerned.

After my parents and brother searched the area, my mother approached the announcer's office to request a missing children alert over the speaker system. However, her request was denied because they said it wouldn't be heard over the noise of the crowd.

By this time, my parents were frantic and searched the grounds behind the oval, the car parks, stands ... everywhere in the vicinity of the oval. By the time the announcer agreed to raise the alert (an hour after their disappearance), the football game had finished, and the crowds had begun dispersing.

The girls were officially reported missing to the police that afternoon.

Forty-nine years have lapsed since that day, and despite numerous appeals, a million-dollar reward, alleged sightings, alleged suspects, possible evidence, both Joanne and Kirste have never been located, nor has anyone ever been charged for their kidnapping and suspected homicide.

Born 14 months after Joanne disappeared, I grew up in her shadow and was denied the opportunity of knowing her personally and having a sister. As a toddler, I was curious about the little girl in the photos on our mantlepiece. I would often ask, 'Why is she in the photos? Why isn't she here playing with me? Why, why, why ....'

My family were patient and gently answered my questions with the simplest of explanations to not confuse me. And as I grew older, my questions became more intense, the answers more complex.

Some nights, after everyone else had gone to bed, I would sit in the darkness of the loungeroom and talk to Joanne in her photo. Sometimes, I would hear Mum and Dad crying, though they clearly did their best to conceal their tears from David and me.

For many years after the girls disappeared, Dad searched for them in his spare time. As a bread carter, he would leave early in the morning, complete his shift delivering bread through the Adelaide Hills, then return home to shower, change his clothes and pick up a packed meal from Mum, before setting out in hope of finding something, anything, that would help to find the girls. He never did find that something, and he eventually succumbed to pancreatic cancer in 1981. On his deathbed, Dad pleaded for someone to come forward, and to never forget the Adelaide Oval abductions.

Thankfully, my father's deathbed plea to the public to never forget the girls was answered, especially in South Australia, where their abduction is remembered to this day. This was important to Dad, not only for the memory of the girls, but for public safety. The kidnapper, after all, was still 'out there' and possibly preying on other children.

My childhood was a lot different to that of others. My family was extremely protective. My every step was watched, be that by my mum, my dad, David, or family friends. I couldn't go anywhere unless someone was escorting me, and it felt so unfair. Although I didn't become rebellious, I did become argumentative, determined to get under Mum's skin. And while my amazing mum never told me in so many words, I am sure there were times when she could have happily sent me off to boarding school!

In 1986, at the age of 11, Mum decided we would leave Adelaide and move to Coober Pedy – a small outback opal mining town in the far north of South Australia. Unbeknown to me at that time, Mum was terrified that history would repeat itself and she would lose her other 11-year-old daughter if we stayed in Adelaide. Mum, however, kept this fear to herself for many years.

Coober Pedy is a small town, where people who wish to escape their history, to make a new start, or begin a whole new life move to, and in effect, it became somewhat of a saviour for our family. I was able to spend time with friends, ride my bike out to the local creek, spend hours away without a watchful eye. In Adelaide, we were 'the family of one of the little girls abducted from the Adelaide Oval'. In Coober Pedy, we were just other residents. Although some people knew our family past, they minded their own business, unless Mum wanted to talk about it. After all, they had their own past hiding in their closets.

Each family of a missing person handles their emotions differently. David found it incredibly difficult and often hid inside his shell, reluctant to talk about Joanne and her disappearance. David and Joanne were as thick as thieves. Wherever there was mischief, Joanne or David would be at the head of it, with the other in the wake. They shared a love and sibling bond that others would covet. David passed away in April 2020, and to his final day, he blamed himself for not protecting Joanne, as he always had while growing up.

Words can't describe how much my mother has inspired me. Over ten years, Mum lost not only her daughter, but her own mother, grandmother, sister, brother, husband, and then her father. Did these losses break her? No. They made her stronger. My mum's mantra to the day she died was, 'Keep putting one foot in front of the other, and if you stumble and fall, pick yourself up, brush yourself off and keep going. There are people a hell of a lot worse off than us.'

Given *all* that Mum had lost, her resilience continues to motivate me to be my best version of me. I know that Mum, Dad, David *and* Joanne wouldn't want me to be another victim of the tragedy. They'd want me to have a life filled with happiness and meaning. So, each day I am grateful to be alive and grateful for the resilience that my mother modelled for me. I look for reasons to be thankful and always find them.

Another tool that gives me peace is acceptance of what I can't change. My sister was kidnapped, and so I had a choice as to how I wished to deal with it. Did I let the tragedy consume and destroy me, or did I want to create a life with happiness and meaning that my family would want for me?

I've chosen happiness. With my loving partner and my angel-hearted daughter, Tamara, I've created a new family. Every day, I consciously model to Tamara what my mother modelled for me – to rise again and again.

Another major key to my resilience is a profound sense of purpose. Joanne and Kriste are just two of *thousands* of missing people whose stories are forgotten, whose families are as lost as their loved ones, fighting to have their stories told. After connecting with a couple of these families, I wanted to use my family's high profile to shine a light on their loved ones and ensure they are never forgotten.

In 2015, I established Leave a Light On Inc. to raise awareness of missing persons cases in Australia. From our tragedies, we created a beacon of hope and support. By working alongside other missing persons organisations, we promote long-term cases and raise awareness of the need for ongoing support for families and friends dealing with the ambiguous loss of a missing person.

After Joanne disappeared, my parents would leave the front porch light on, in hope that if Joanne ever found her way home, she would see that we were there waiting for her. Although my parents and David have since passed away, my front porch light still shines bright, a symbol of hope that we can guide those who are missing back home. Every year on 21 October, we encourage people to leave a light on in memory of those missing. Be it a front porch light, an indoor light, or a candle – we want to symbolically brighten missing persons' paths home.

Ambiguous loss is like no other. There are no answers, no end to the grief, a life in limbo, a nightmare you never wake up from. There are no guides or easy steps to deal with the unknown and navigate the plethora of emotions we feel: anguish, grief, sorrow, heartbreak, anger, frustration and indifference. Then come the questions. Are they safe, are they well, are they alive, are they suffering? Our eyes search the crowds, reading papers, social media, television coverages, all for the possible glimpse they may be out there. Media is our greatest friend, but also our worst enemy. Headlines such as 'remains located, police to identify remains' suspend our breath. We wonder, *is this our day?* However, we hope it isn't, for deep down we want our loved one to be alive and walk back through our front door.

In Australia, there are currently over 2600 long-term missing persons. These cases are defined as someone who has been reported to police as having their whereabouts unknown and there are fears for their safety or concern for their welfare. A person can go missing for a variety of reasons, including misadventure, mental illness, domestic violence, miscommunication or, as in the case of Joanne and Kirste, a victim of crime. One of our key public education messages is that you don't have to wait 24 hours before you report someone missing. In fact, early reporting of a missing loved one is advantageous to finding them.

Nothing ever prepares you for the experience of an ambiguous loss, and it can happen to anyone at any time. I was blessed to have Kath Ratcliffe as my mother for, through her resilience, I have developed my own resilience, which has enabled me to support and strengthen others.

Sometimes life throws hand grenades at you that test your resilience. Currently, I am battling cancer with chemotherapy, which has knocked me down more than I expected. Whenever I feel sorry for myself, I hear Mum's voice say, 'Come on, Suzie, one foot at a time ....'

Mum's legacy carries me forward, and I hope it helps to carry you too.

Chapter 15

Flying Free

Tanya Heaslip

Rising from boarding school trauma.

'Stuffing pain down doesn't make pain go away.
It eventually bubbles up through the cracks.
It wants to come to the light to be healed.'

I grew up in outback Central Australia on a cattle station in the 1960s and early 70s. Every part of my world was magical – freedom, space, huge blue skies, rocky red ranges, wild animals. I was a free-spirited daydreamer, happiest with my books and wandering through the bush alone, telling stories to myself. I was also the eldest child, looking after a younger sister and two brothers. We did Correspondence School and School of the Air, and I loved it all.

From a young age, my siblings and I also worked in the stock camp alongside the stockmen and were an integral part of the station workforce. It was tough mustering cattle in 45-degree Celsius heat, eking out tiny sips of water from the water bag on a saddle to avoid perishing, stuck in the dust behind the mob on the endless drive to get them back to water before nightfall. The mantras of our childhood were: 'never give up' and 'there's no such word as can't.'

Dad taught us to suck a rock to keep moisture in our dust-coated, parched mouths during long droving days. He reminded us constantly that 'Drinking too much water makes you soft.' Softness was a sin in the desert. You could die from softness, in less than a day.

We learnt these lessons young and were proud of our toughness. Our lives had meaning and purpose. And I never felt safer and happier than when in the bush.

Life events that followed, however, were far tougher than the physical challenges of my childhood. Aged 12, I was sent 1600 kilometres away from home to boarding school in Adelaide, South Australia.

Almost all outback children were sent to boarding school because secondary school options weren't available in the bush. I knew it was coming, but nothing could have prepared me for the reality.

Boarding school was far from the jolly hockey sticks romp that Enid Blyton had written about in *Malory Towers* and *The Twins at St Clare's*. There were no kind mistresses, brave and wise prefects, fun dormitories, and larks with chums that I'd read about in my School of the Air library books.

Boarding school was prison. And in this prison, as in the military, there was a system. They took the individual and broke them down, systematically removing all individual traits until that person was just part of a mass where everyone conformed.

Boarding school stripped us of all rights. We were run by rules, bells, tunics, stone walls, grey skies, and constant punishment administered by pinch-faced, tight-lipped mistresses.

Walking, running, talking, being in the wrong place at the wrong time, not having my top button properly buttoned up, not having my bed properly made, not following the shower roster properly, not standing in line respectfully enough, not standing to attention appropriately – the rules covered our every breathing moment. A handheld bell clanged to wake us, and those bells ruled the day until we were clanged upstairs to bed. There was no kindness, no pastoral care, there was just the ever-present threat of punishment.

The punishments were not as bad as in the military or a prison, I grant you – we weren't physically beaten – but the punishments were degrading, designed to shame. They included having to stand alone in the mistress's office while the mistresses watched us as we cleaned all the shoes of all the girls, or being sent to solitary confinement in sickbay for three days, or being refused parental access (if ever a parent happened to visit), and being regularly 'gated' – locked in the school, forbidden from going out (assuming you had some family or approved friends to go out with). Girls were regularly even told they had been sent to boarding school because their parents no longer loved them.

My mother discovered the hard way that it wasn't just her daughter who'd lost her freedom and her rights. So had she. The headmistress refused to take Mum's phone calls or respond to her desperate pleas when I wrote tear-smudged letters home, desperately seeking help. I was tiny, with no social skills, easy prey for the bullies, but there was no one to save me. And coming home was not an option.

The situation was worse for my beloved sister when she came to boarding school the following year. A group of nameless girls held her head down in a soiled toilet and then left her on the floor, sobbing, hair and face full of faeces and urine. I was helpless, I couldn't make it better. Siblings were kept apart. It was all part of the 'breaking down the former life' process. She could only whisper her experiences to me a day later, when we secretly met behind the toilets. She was still sobbing, shaking, traumatised.

When the Methodist minister thundered every Sunday that we were sinners, my sense of hopelessness deepened. I buckled, went under, hid the shame and despair deep inside. I also stuffed down the suffocation and terror of being trapped, imprisoned, and never able to escape – because it was easier than crying every night. Yet the ache and misery for home and safety of family hung in my heart like a heavy stone of unshed tears.

It wasn't easy for my parents either, but they had sent us

away to give us a better life, an education, new opportunities. Their generosity and courage gave me something powerful to draw upon, along with the lessons I'd learnt on the back of a horse.

Mum would always say that 'hurdles are something to just jump over'. And Dad would recite the 'bullock story' when things got tough. 'After a long day mustering, you finally get the bullocks back to the yards. Then some fool leaves the gate open, and the bullocks escape overnight.' He'd pause for full effect, because when that happened, we all knew the world had come to an end. 'But there's nothing you can do, so get in your swag, have a good night's sleep, put your boots on tomorrow, and go out and get the cattle in all over again.'

So – no complaining, no despair. Just put one foot in front of the other. And get on with it. No matter the hardship, just focus on getting the cattle back, and then to the dam for water. Never give up.

My wonderful School of the Air teacher, Mrs Hodder, had given me a toolkit for survival, too. She had taught us creativity through song, storytelling and reading aloud over the wireless. So, I played my guitar at boarding school and taught the boarders to sing country songs along with me. They were the Slim Dusty, Charley Pride, and Olivia Newton-John ballads I'd learnt around the campfire with the stockmen. Singing them reminded me of who I once was – strong, free and happy.

And at nights before lights out, the girls would crowd around the end of my bed and I'd tell them stories of growing up in the bush – galloping along on my horse, back at a time and place when I felt strong and whole and of value. Then

I'd write the stories down and read them aloud to the girls again.

The sisterhood – my fellow boarders – became my family. In the absence of mothers, family life, or any kind of love in our lives at school, we supported each other, and we are still deeply bonded to this day. Such a precious thing.

Study also saved me. I threw myself into academic learning, the music of the school, and discovering how to contribute back. I ultimately became a boarding house prefect because of my determination to make something of the experience. And at the end of a further five years, I graduated from law school, the first School of the Air student to do so. University wasn't something that had ever happened for anyone in my family. It was an enormous privilege.

I have since learnt that survival is an inbuilt human instinct.

Equally, we must find meaning in what we do, to have hope for the next part of our journey, to make this life worthwhile.

My hero, Victor Frankl, argued in his book *Man's Search for Meaning* that hope is the most important human need. It was hope that kept him alive while suffering unspeakable atrocities in a German concentration camp.

And while holding onto hope, you must keep digging deep and trusting that the sunshine will finally come again. As my dear nana always said, 'This too will pass.'

Over the years, I have practised wrapping hope around the big picture of a problem and finding the silver lining or overall benefit, even in tough times.

It works – because hope is a happy thing.

For me, it always begins with a surge of excitement in the heart, the enticing sense that something is possible despite the odds and painting a picture in my mind of what it could look like. I write it down; sometimes I even draw pictures. I try to use all the senses to give it the best possible basis to come into form. A sense of hope for something better, bigger, always strives me forward.

It has led me into challenging legal roles, where I've needed every bit of that hope. The legal world was patriarchal and misogynistic, and the practise of law made mustering cattle look easy. Vomiting before going into court, trembling before a judge, struggling to control brain freeze while making submissions – those early years were tough. Luckily, I'd grown up with stockmen and could work as hard as anyone, and I determinedly carved out my own successes.

Yet despite this, I wanted to fly free, see the world, taste it, explore it. I wanted to write stories about it and the people I met and their journeys.

This longing and hope for something more in my life led me to backpack solo through Western Europe in 1989. There I watched the miracle of the Berlin Wall fall and returned to Australia clutching a piece of wall hacked out for me by an East German soldier. I was fascinated about what lay over the other side of that Wall and ended up in the Czech Republic, teaching English to the Minister of Justice and the judges of the High Court, just four years after communism had fallen.

My time there didn't start well either, and I had to draw on every one of my inner strengths to get through. I was teaching English in an industrial city called Sedlčany, a Cold War setting where time had not moved on. People in the streets wouldn't look at me. I was defined by the West, and not welcome. I couldn't read or understand a word of Czech. The place was so badly polluted by brown smog that my respiratory system collapsed. I feared ending up in a Russian gulag or Siberian salt mine where my family would never find me.

But always, always, there were people of kindness and goodwill, and they helped me survive. As did recalling the inner tools I'd used to get through my childhood and boarding school experiences. And then I found fairytale Prague, and my life changed forever.

My time in Eastern Europe at such a difficult time of political transition opened my eyes wider and expanded my understanding of life. I learnt to let go of expectations and embrace all that was new in the adventure lying before me: the beauty of its ancient architecture, soul-soaring music, the rise and fall of lyrical language. I was humbled and uplifted by this magical, complicated country.

I've never had a comfort zone. Mostly, I've leapt, darted and frog-leapt from challenge to challenge, always seeking the next big adventure. Thanks to the legacy of boarding school, I've fought against anything that might 'tie me down'.

Over the years, my restless, hungry approach to life led to many different types of law: Junior Instructing Solicitor for the Lindy Chamberlain Inquiry; decades of civil litigation and court work; freelancing and consulting across Australia; and finally in-house general counsel roles, where I've supported and encouraged other female lawyers to fight the 'glass ceiling'. My inner drive has always been to make things better for people who are struggling, and there is no comfort zone in that. However, there is satisfaction when I can make things better, even if just for one person.

And after years away, I have finally returned home to live on the red soil of Central Australia. My restless soul has once again found its place amongst the rocky ranges and blue skies and freedom of the outback.

Here I've also been able to write three books of my dreams: *An Alice Girl* – about my childhood in the outback; *Beyond Alice* – about the boarding school years; and *Alice to Prague* – about those adventures. Writing has been healing in so many ways.

And I've been supported by my wonderful husband, mother and sister, who understand my need for creativity and the power of drawing deep on my foundations.

If I can add any words of inspiration, know this: you are not alone. Seek help. For decades I drowned under the deep, dark weight of disconnection and anxiety, the lack of self-esteem and poor choices, and boarding school nightmares that never went away. I blamed myself, thinking there was something wrong with me. It took me years to work out there wasn't. I wish I'd understood that earlier and sought help. But like most people, I was ashamed and tried to hide my darkness. I covered it up with being a 'good-time party girl' and pretended I was Pollyanna when things got tough. Or I hid under blankets. Sometimes that worked, sometimes it didn't.

It took a long time to learn that stuffing pain down doesn't make pain go away. It eventually bubbles up through the cracks. It wants to come to the light to be healed.

So, my advice is: be bold, bring it out into the sunshine, make peace with it and let it go. We have one life, and I am now determined to recreate mine on my terms.

Then rewrite your own script – of who and what you want to be for your future years! Visualise it, affirm it, dream it, and learn to be your own best friend. Embrace coincidences, serendipity, opportunities – follow them, open your heart. We only have one life.

Dad was a pilot, and he would say, 'A plane can only take off *into* the wind.'

So, open your wings and learn to fly!

Chapter 16

Smile and Sing

Sally Herzfeld

Rising to my challenges as a 1950s and 60s teacher in outback Australia.

'A smile is one of the simplest ways to lighten your day and that of everyone you encounter.'

When I was born in 1935, I was named Alison, which changed to Al to Ally … to Sally, which somehow stuck.

I grew up near Perth, Western Australia, and experienced a happy childhood despite the background of World War Two. In summer, we would go to outdoor movies to watch cartoons, which were followed by horrible war news. I still have a vivid memory of a nightmare when I jumped out of bed screaming that fierce soldiers were coming over the hill with swords drawn. My happiest war memory though is that of my brother running down to the church and ringing the bell because we had heard on the news that the war was over! Our uncle and our friends' dads would be coming home.

I was one of five children whose parents were driven largely by their strong humanitarian values. They found many channels to help improve the lives of other people – from organisations that supported Aboriginal and Torres Strait Islander people's welfare, and the United Nations, to the Quakers and other local organisations. With the same drive instilled in me, I was a keen Girl Guide and proudly achieved the highest achievable award – Queen's Guide Award – when I was 15 years old.

I loved primary school, and by the age of ten, my career path to teaching was set.

In 1956, when I was 20 years old, I was a qualified teacher and excited to embark on my first teaching appointment at the Forrest River Mission for Aboriginal families near Wyndham, in the far north of Western Australia. It is also known as one of the hottest places in Australia and now called Oombulgurri.

Being a hot, tropical area, it was well populated by bugs,

snakes and crocodiles. I shot snakes, poisoned cockroaches that tickled when I sat on the splintery toilet seat and had a close encounter with a crocodile that nearly landed in our little boat. Sandflies were prolific, and scratching their bites caused infections. And let's not forget the hookworm!

While the animals and bugs were largely hostile, the Aboriginal people were friendly and welcoming. Their culture was a mixture of Anglican and traditional beliefs. They would go to church every Sunday and practise their cultural ways, such as corroboree dancing and having skin names that controlled who they could marry. The old people lived in camps outside the compound so they could be more traditional. The tribe embraced me like I was part of the family. I joined in corroborees, was taken bush to live off bush tucker and taught much about their culture, which I treasure to this day.

The temperature would sometimes soar up to 45 degrees Celsius, with high humidity, and be not much cooler at night. Airconditioning didn't exist, of course. We slept inside mosquito nets, usually under our houses, which were on stilts. We swam in freshwater holes, for the freshwater crocs weren't as deadly as the 'salties'. We had kerosene fridges, hessian safes for food storage, and we ate a lot of tinned food, plus anything we grew or caught. A steer was killed about every week for the whole mission.

Our two-teacher, single classroom had waist-high straw walls around it with a good space between them and the roof to let a breeze drift through. There was no electricity in the schoolhouse or our personal houses, so we relied on the generator for power, which was only turned on for a couple of hours for light during the evenings.

Evening entertainment for me was mainly singing at church, marking exams and preparing for lessons, writing letters, listening to my battery wireless or playing board games with children unless I had any special adult friends. I also did a lot of embroidery and dressmaking.

My greatest challenge was not the deadly animals, nor the isolation, nor heat. It was some of the other staff at the Mission. The other schoolteacher had been there for a year before me and was disappointed that the government sent a 'first year out' teacher. My welcome to my first school was therefore … underwhelming, and she would often take her disappointment out on me. 'What would you know about that?' she would say.

My colleague often used a cane to beat the children. In contrast, I had been taught by my parents and Teachers' College that if you hit a child, you had failed. As there was only one classroom, our classes sat back-to-back, and we teachers would watch each other's different teaching styles. Each time a student was caned, it wasn't only that child who suffered. Everyone in the room was sad and frightened that it might happen to them.

When it was appropriate for the lesson, I enjoyed taking my students outside, away from my colleague, into nature where we could use everyday, natural material for learning.

Staffing for the rest of the Mission was a challenge too. During my two years there, there was an influx of new staff who varied in suitability. Like many people who came to the 'never, never', some were escaping from their past and unprepared for the isolation or weather conditions, and many weren't happy with the situation! Others were troublemaking 'do-gooders' who came with rigid opinions about how to 'fix things' without understanding the whole picture or appreciating the opinions of those who were more experienced.

I witnessed numerous heated arguments with the Mission staff and found the tension and hostility from them overwhelming. Afterall, I was there to teach, not to sort out or put up with 'white fella disagreements'! In the worst times, I would find places to hide and cry – a muddy river or in bed at night, where others couldn't see me. In those days, showing one's fragility or sadness wasn't encouraged, but I always felt a little better after a good cry. Looking for and recognising the good attributes and behaviours in the staff was also helpful.

Two years later, in 1959, I accepted a job in the north-western town of Port Hedland, Western Australia. There, I taught a large group of young Aboriginal children in a rusty old shed during the day, and then their parents one evening per week. The men wanted to learn to read and write and do useful maths, and the women wanted to sew with hand machines.

This community was called the Pindan Mob. While they maintained solid cultural practices, they were also enterprising. They started the Pindan Co-operative Business, which collected minerals, built fibreglass boats, made stock whips, collected pearl shells, kept chooks and goats for food and fished. Some of them also thought it best to stay out of town because of unhealthy influences such as alcohol, gambling, prostitution, flirting with someone of the wrong skin name, and stealing.

Others wanted their children to be educated at school, which was in town. This meant that some children lived away from their families for schooling. I remember feeling sorry for those students because family bonds were strong in those communities.

Another challenge I faced as a teacher was the Aboriginal people's fear that their children would be taken away from them – the impact of the stolen generation. In 1960, I wanted my students to join in an interschool sports carnival in Wittenoom Gorge. This meant sleeping there for at least two nights. A female leader persuaded the rest of the mob that we might steal the children, so it didn't happen.

The next year, I tried again. I explained to her how the trip would work, when the children would return and what a great opportunity it would be for them. Like a receipt, I made a list of all the children's names, with her name and the date on top. She agreed but told me firmly that she would be counting each child when they returned.

Months later, a group of angry Pindan leaders stormed over to my house, showing me that list of names and demanded to know why I had given permission for those children to be taken away. When I explained the list was for a sports carnival, they all laughed and drove off.

Racism was not uncommon in those days. One day, we received notice that there was going to be a children's fancy-dress party in town. A few days before the event, one of the organisers said it would be better if my students didn't go. *My* students were deemed to have runny noses, swear too much, were smelly, or do inappropriate sexual things. This was like a red rag to a bull! I knew that none of these things would be the case, so I ignored the organisers and helped the children get ready for the event. The big boys went as corroboree men, and the girls dressed up as their favourite book characters. Everyone had a great time. Non-Indigenous parents even complimented our children and apologised for their prejudiced comments made before the event.

Facing problems as challenges to overcome really does work! I always say to myself, 'Come on, Sal! You CAN do it!'

Life as an outback teacher back then was far from easy, but the values and lessons that I fostered as a child gave me a strong foundation to cope with challenges and thrive. The Quaker philosophy of answering 'to that of God' in everyone was particularly helpful. Because there is the light of God in every living being, everyone has within them the potential for goodness.

There is a lot of power in words that we say and think. What a difference it makes to a child when they hear words of praise, instead of criticism. Equally, the words we say to ourselves make a difference. I therefore prefer to speak to myself and to others kindly.

I often also lean on some of the Girl Guide principles to strengthen my resilience. At the very heart of Girl Guides is a commitment to help others in need, and in doing so, we 'smile and sing under all difficulties'. This doesn't mean *always* smiling like a clown. As I said earlier, sometimes a good cry can be helpful. However, just as there is power in words, there is power in smiling. Smiling makes you feel better and the people around you. A smile is one of the simplest ways to lighten your day and that of everyone you encounter.

Relationships with people were vital to my resilience. Writing letters to my family and friends at home and receiving them was always exciting. Now, of course, we use email, which is instant. How times have changed.

Having fun with the children was something I did naturally with them, and looking back, I can see that it was another resilience tool. We used to laugh often, in and out of the classroom, and we played many games.

Over the years, I also learnt to trust my intuition. When I think about something deeply and feel it is right, I tap into my inner strength and act accordingly, even when others may disagree with me. I follow my intuition, while also being empathetic with people who might disagree with me. I may not always make the right decisions, and if the outcome is disappointing, I take responsibility and learn a lesson. Regardless of the outcome of my decisions, I choose them and wear the consequences.

Rising to my calling as an outback teacher in the 1950s and 60s was achievable because my childhood prepared me with fundamental resilience skills. Moreover, I loved the adventure, felt gratitude for my experiences and genuinely loved my students and wanted to help them through a good education. When you rise to adventure, there are always rewards to be gained.

When I was teaching in Port Hedland, a young civil engineer was checking equipment on the other side of the shed. He saw this skinny white girl doing corroboree dancing with Aboriginal children and recorded it on his tape recorder. He invited me to dinner that evening to hear it, and we have been together for 63 years.

Today, my husband and I have a multicultural family with children, grand and great grandchildren. I am in contact with my ex-students who are still alive, and I recently gifted them my book, *Outback Teacher*.

In 1971, my husband and I bought a block of land with a classroom on it in the hills near Perth. From there, we created Helena College – a non-denominational private school that integrated children with special needs, encouraging them to do their best rather than being better than anyone else, and we fostered care and compassion for all life on Earth through membership of the Save the Children Fund and the Gould League Nature Club. The college quickly grew to approximately 800 students who ranged from three years old to eighteen. I am still involved with the school, local community groups, and Quakers.

Although I was only in my twenties when I set off to teach in one of Australia's hottest and harshest environments, I was aware that the challenges were good for my personal growth and character. Had I stayed near Perth in the comfort of familiar surrounds, my life would have been unfulfilled and incomplete. I relished the challenge, despite the hardship.

My advice for a good life is to take on challenges. Look for adventures, for it is in challenges and adventures that we grow. Take care of yourself. Eat healthy food. Try to be positive and think about what is going well for you, even though there is plenty that isn't. Seek advice from professionals if necessary and find someone or some others to help in some way.

Chapter 17

The Miracle of Love

Ondine Sherman

Rising to my unexpected challenges as a mother.

'Highest on the workout regime is gratitude, gratitude and more gratitude. Beyond a cheesy hashtag, it truly works.'

I think back at life *before*, on the day I squeezed my daughter Jasmine's hand as she skipped down the street, singing a sweet song, fairy wings flapping over her stripy shirt and leggings. At nearly two, with a shaggy fringe and soft curls, she was beyond adorable and inspired smiles from even the grumpiest passers-by.

We arrived at our local café, and I ordered her favourite – a hot chocolate. It was time for my afternoon coffee, and I pulled Jasmine onto my lap, navigating the wings, and wedged her slightly sideways against my growing pregnant tummy. I dug a picture book out of my bag – of fairies, of course – and sneaked a kiss into the crook of her neck. Endorphins rushed, and I thanked the heavens for the gorgeous little girl I had always dreamt of.

I was also waiting, with increasing anxiety, for my twins. I didn't know if they would be a boy or girl, or two of each. Like many expecting mothers with a career, my main concern was how I'd navigate my way with three children under three, while maintaining my dream job – co-managing Voiceless, the animal protection institute – as I didn't want to miss work too long. Voiceless was an organisation my dad and I built together, and it meant the world to me. Protecting animals was my life's mission, and I had known it in my bones since I was a child. My husband, Dror, reassured me that we'd make it work. He'd help and reduce his hours in his post-Doctoral research project, if needed.

Two years later, on one evening at 10 pm, the bombshell email from the laboratory in Chicago arrived. Results confirmed that my identical twin boys had an ultra-rare genetic disorder that projected severe lifelong disabilities. Dov and Lev, the specialist said, would not be able to walk, feed themselves, use the toilet, talk, and may need a feeding tube. There was no cure, no research even, as only 200 cases around the world had been diagnosed.

All my previous worries about my career, my work-life balance dissipated. In its place was sheer terror and bone-deep grief coupled with a panic so intense I often felt disassociated from my body and mind. I'd see myself talking, moving, smiling, and know I wasn't there. I was, in my reality, hanging by my fingernails on a cliff face with an abyss below. *I am about to fall and won't survive.*

Years of medical appointments, therapists and specialists beat much of the denial and hope out of Dror and me.

Why did this happen to me? 'It's not fair,' I yelled to no one. I had tried hard to be a good person.

My life was insanely busy taking care of my twins, with often twice or thrice-daily therapies because early intervention 'was crucial'. And I was worried about Jasmine – from coming with us to doctor and therapist appointments, inevitably listening to adult conversations about medical treatments and hopes for cures (later to be dashed), bringing home new friends and navigating their awkwardness when first meeting Dov and Lev, to helping push their wheelchairs in a mall, cinema or airport and feeling the stares of passers-by.

I had understood, after reading countless articles, that siblings often acquire emotional and behavioural problems due to feeling abandoned, ashamed, guilty, resentful, and obligated to take on an active carer role from a young age. So, I tried hard to protect her, ensure her life was joyful and full, with lots of activities, playdates at our house (to make sure she always felt comfortable having friends over) and regular mummy-and-me time.

Friends and relatives wanted to help me, to support, but nobody knew how. It felt like there was nothing to be done. Nothing anyone could do.

I thought I knew what 'people' were saying. I felt their stares on the street, the pointing children and awkward mothers pulling them away. *Oh, the tragedy.* The pity. Attitudes also came through in people's questions, some of which made me tremble with fury. I had never noticed, never had cause to pay attention to, the prejudice towards people with disabilities in our society. How disability is viewed not as diversity but tragedy. Rather than community support enveloping special-needs families with love and services, these families are considered a drain on the economy, something to screen out. 'Didn't you do pregnancy tests?' became a regular question from acquaintances and even strangers. After a while, I understood this to mean, 'How can I (or my sister, my daughter) avoid this disorder/prevent your life from happening to me/not fall into your hellhole?'

My future was, as I saw it, a black hole. An abyss with stolen, broken expectations of a life well-lived, of a happy family.

And eventually, I retreated inside myself.

The guilt was all-encompassing, and I told myself, *I must try more, do more, be more. Increase the therapies, practise harder, retrain myself as a therapist, re-design their diet as organic, gluten-free, no-sugar, high-protein or ...? Give up my career and selfish pursuits so I can be available to them 24 hours a day, seven days a week.*

I tried to work but found I couldn't be effective, as I was a shadow. When the tears arrived, I started therapy, terrified I would lose myself so profoundly that I'd never find a way back.

And, as I always did when I faced troubles in life, I started to read: religious books, philosophical treatises, memoirs of lives derailed.

I also began to take a notebook wherever I went. After dropping Jasmine at kindergarten, while waiting for her at ballet class, in between Dov and Lev's therapies, while walking my dogs … I'd find moments to sit, minutes to scribble dark thoughts, selfish thoughts. The shame I felt. I wrote down the black future, the life I would never realise, images of my twins graduating, of family holidays, making sandcastles on the beach. And the life to come, the wheelchairs, the adult nappies, the never-ending stares, the aching backs from lifting.

Slowly, I found refuge in a small list of nourishments: therapy, journalling, long walks with my dogs, music and yoga. I continued to read other people's stories of loss, disease and disability. Their resilience spoke to me as I turned the pages and gave me hope that I may find my own.

Sometimes, at the end of a yoga class, I'd have to wipe off mascara from my cheeks as it had run down from my tears. Or, on a walk, my dogs would wait patiently as I sobbed in a hidden corner of a park. I realised, just as deep into sadness as I dive, I emerge into the air to breathe again. Gradually, notebooks full, I created structure, began chapters. I started to write a book: *The Miracle of Love*, to air my laundry, to process my story through telling it. Later, I realised this is called 'bibliotherapy'.

Today, 16 years later, all my worst fears have been realised. I drive the disability van fitted for two wheelchairs. I tick off adult diapers from my shopping list. My house revolves with therapists and helpers, giving little privacy, which is tough for an introvert. I haven't showed my boys the elephants of Africa and delighted in their awe, as my parents did with me. Dror has never kicked a ball with them in the park, as he dreamed of, his own little football team. Jasmine's not a ball-fan either.

I fell off that cliff and landed below, injured with pain, shame and sadness. But slowly my wounds healed, my heart mended, and I looked around. I saw sunlight making wildflowers sparkle. I felt the soft touch of Jasmine's cheek when I kissed her. And I heard the deep belly laughs of Dov and Lev as they splashed in the pool. My happy children.

Although I hadn't expected this dream to be mine, my family is everything I've ever wanted. I adore my three children beyond words, and they don't seem to mind me either. Dror and I have loved each other since I was nineteen. We've walked through fire and, although a little crispy, we stand side-by-side. Family and friends, the real ones, have stayed close. Once I started to express myself, they listened and heard. I ranted about our lack of respect for people with disabilities in our society and found people who agreed, who are trying to create change. I returned to my animal protection organisation, to my soul-work, with a new perspective, kinder and wiser.

Dov and Lev, although they look almost indistinguishable, have vastly different interests. I play guitar with Dov, helping him to strum. He's super picky about the songs we sing. I help Lev flip through the photo albums he loves returning to. Dov delights in mixing paint colours with an occasional stroke on paper; Lev wins the hearts of neighbours in his daily wheelchair walks. Through their touch-screen computers, they tell us they feel like pasta for dinner and request their favourite TV show.

Jasmine is now 18 and has graduated high school. She continues to beam her light, still making the grumpiest passers-by smile in admiration. She's kind, confident, smart, funny and self-assured. Growing up with two disabled brothers hasn't been easy for her. But, although tough to handle, it has perhaps heightened her empathy, strengthened her resilience and given her tools for life that will stand her in good stead for challenges ahead. At least I hope so.

My work-life balance is tricky to maintain, as it is with so many of us women. But I have a toolbox of strategies to keep my chin held high. I make time for self-care and exhaling guilt. I surround myself with people who are authentic and open-hearted.

Every day, I practise mantras, movements and meditations, to keep me here in the present, grateful for everything I have. I'm not prone to advice-giving, but if I did, apart from a good therapist, I would recommend three things that worked for me ....

Firstly, daily practices to train your mind. Like any muscle (and I'm certainly not an exercise guru), our emotional brain can be strengthened in positive ways. Highest on the workout regime is gratitude, gratitude and more gratitude. Beyond a cheesy hashtag, it truly works. Sometimes this means forcing yourself to spell it out, write it down daily. *I am grateful for ...* and then list ten things. Even if you're so down that all you can think of is the smallest of things, a flowering tree, warm hug ... a juicy peach. I still practise it often, especially when I'm blue.

Secondly, to avoid the overwhelming fear of what *could* happen, things out of my control, I worked hard to catch my future-focused anxious thoughts and release them gently out the window. I made a zero-tolerance rule – no worrying about the 'black' future, which included no answering questions on that issue from well-meaning people (*What will happen when …?)* which always spiralled me. Sometimes I do slip up and begin to fret, but most of the time, my inner fearmonger knows it will be shooshed.

Lastly, finding times in the day for the smallest activities that give you joy. Of course, this is different for each person. They can be quick, cheap and easy. I'm not talking about heading to a resort in Hawaii or even spending a day at the spa, but simple pleasures like making a new playlist (and then singing out loud or even enjoying a quick solo pyjama dance!) A ten-minute walk on the beach, a free yoga class, courtesy of YouTube, or a long bath with a good book … whatever floats your boat.

From my experience, the grand gestures of life aren't helpful, but the tiniest sparks, those that light up our inner selves, remind us that we're still us and they make us feel human again. Those sparks that, day by day, month by month, lead us slowly back to a bright, contented life. A joyful life. A life to be truly grateful for.

Photo by Artem Kovalev

Chapter 18

My Patchwork Life

Sandy Sullivan

Rising from domestic violence and homelessness.

Names and details of this story have been changed for legal and safety reasons.

'I have come through the other side of abuse and homelessness as a different woman. A stronger, wiser and resilient woman.'

Chronic stomach pain was the reason I called the ambulance, yet they ended up rushing me to hospital with multiple leg fractures because while stumbling around in the dark to greet the paramedics, I had tripped over my bike and broke my leg in three places! After months of healing, I was literally getting back on my feet. Trained and qualified as a fitness instructor, I had my own business, great clients, and a rental apartment. I was quietly proud of my achievements and happy.

In 2015, I gave up my apartment to move in with a guy that I'd only known for a few weeks. I was swept off my feet and fell for him. Three weeks later, he snatched my car keys from my hand to stop me from driving away. The violence spiralled into a nightmare that I imagined *other* people lived in. Not me.

Eighteen months on, I resolved to leave him at the earliest safe opportunity and prepared my emergency escape bag with cash, identification, crisis support contact numbers, an old phone, essential toiletries and clothes.

One day, when he was in a 'mood', I ducked to avoid his hit.

It was a pivotal moment. Run or be hurt – again.

So, I ran, grabbed the bag and fled to my car, which was parked underground. Trembling, I locked myself in the car and flew out of the car park. Sweating palms, racing heart, my eyes constantly darting to the rear vision mirror, I was terrified he was chasing me.

Turning onto a small main road, my vision was blurred by my tears, and I accidentally accelerated in front of a car that braked to avoid hitting me. I pulled over to the side of the road. Slumping my head on the steering wheel, I shook and sobbed; I was worn out and broken. Someone then knocked on my window, and I slowly lifted my head. A hand indicated to press my window down, so I did. It was the driver of the car behind me.

'Hey, are you ok?' he asked.

No. Not ok. I wasn't ok at all.

The driver listened, sympathised, and encouraged me to go to a police station to make a statement, which I did while he patiently waited for me. Although I had planned to sleep in my car that night, he kindly offered for me to stay in a spare room in his parents' house where he lived. I sensed his genuineness, and felt safe, so I agreed.

Our friendship soon developed into a romantic relationship, which was lovely, and his family were welcoming. After a few months with David, however, cracks began to show, and his behaviour became erratic, rude and disrespectful. I thought, *it's bad, but at least he doesn't hit me.* I knew he was under pressure from work and his family, so I felt sorry for him and, aside from that … I loved him and therefore excused his behaviour. We would fight, then make up, fight, make up and repeat. I thought it was a relatively normal relationship, which I now know is not.

Late one afternoon, when I had been living with David for nine months, I started to feel overbearing cramps, which I thought was my old endometriosis flaring up. A visit to the Royal Hobart Hospital revealed that I was pregnant! I always loved children, but because of my history with endometriosis, I expected to not have any of my own. I quickly adjusted to the news and was elated.

David was equally surprised and shared my excitement. For a short while, we blissfully prepared our little nest, but as we discussed our respective ideas for how he/she would be raised, our differences in values and attitudes shone in my face like a dentist's light, and our relationship reverted to its usual, unhealthy way.

Then, late one evening, David's father, who owned the house, walked in and said to me, 'You gotta go. No more being here.' He had enough of our fighting, and I had to leave. David didn't say anything because he knew his father was serious.

Thankfully, I knew where to go and what to do. You see, the last time I was homeless (only a year earlier), I had periods of sleeping in my car for respite from the violence. So, I contacted crisis support organisations, which offered a crisis hotel for me to live in for a week. After that, I was asked if there was anyone else I could stay with. That hurt, because there wasn't. By this stage, I didn't want to stay with anyone. Overwhelmed by shame, I had enough of being told how dumb, stupid or crazy I was, and that my predicament was my fault.

One of my most peaceful short-term crisis places was living in a convent. Dinner was at 5 pm in the main dining room with the other girls and nuns. Bed was at 7 pm and lights out was at 8 pm. We weren't allowed to have any visitors, and our curfew was 5 or 6 pm. I was there for three weeks and grateful for every day.

From there, I moved to a large refuge for women. Some women were pregnant, a few were on drugs or coming off drugs, medication or alcohol. Once I settled into the refuge, I felt quite relaxed and calm. I mostly kept to myself, and if I wanted company, it was always available. All the staff at the refuge were incredibly supportive, and I will never forget how they made me feel that I mattered. Their kindness bared a stark contrast to my family, who knew I was spending Christmas 2017 on my own, pregnant and in a women's refuge – and didn't come to see me. Their abandonment hurt me deeply. I thought, *if my own family can't be bothered with me, I must be worthless.* I don't know how I would have coped during that time if not for the compassionate staff at the refuge.

I then moved into transitional housing just before Charlotte's birth on 15 March 2017. It may sound cliché, but her birth really was the happiest day of my life. When Charlotte was four months old, I returned to the refuge to visit the staff, who were genuinely excited to see us. One of the women gave us a pretty patchwork blanket, which I still treasure. Sometimes, when I look at the patchwork, it reminds me of my life. Lots of pieces held together by thread, but if the thread is cut and pulled, it can quickly unravel and fall apart. Like the blanket, we need to handle our lives gently and with care and share it only with people who respect us.

I am proud to say that my life is now free of stress, crisis, abuse and insecurity. After four years in transitional housing, Charlotte and I moved into a comfortable, rent-subsided house in a leafy, bayside suburb in 2022. There is a local school around the corner and a park and beach down the road. My landlord is a beautiful human, and I still pinch myself that we are here. Occasionally, I worry if we are *really* safe, (a well-worn old track in my brain), but when I soothe myself with the reality that we *are* safe now and it's *over,* I make a new track.

Since 2019, I have been working on a casual basis for four not-for-profit organisations in the social welfare field.

I completed study in community services and can't wait to replace my four jobs with one great full-time job that helps vulnerable women – and earn a consistent income.

While Charlotte and I may not have a big family, or a perfect life, I have come through the other side of abuse and homelessness as a different woman. A stronger, wiser and resilient woman. Children emulate the behaviour and values of their parents. By being who I am today, Charlotte is growing into a compassionate, empathetic and strong little girl.

The trauma of homelessness doesn't just stop once you are housed, but when you do have the security of a home, you can relax and heal in your own time. Sometimes, I'm amazed how I survived the toughest times, but there were certain tools that helped me cope, such as humour. Laughing at myself and being silly, was definitely a coping mechanism.

Journal writing was also good for me. Sometimes, I wrote a list of *things to do*, in priority order. Once I ticked off the list, I would mark it with a giant tick and the word *DONE*. Over time, I ended up with a bank of accomplishments that strengthened my self-confidence and showed I was competent and worthy.

I remember slowing my breathing. It took practise, but the practise paid off. By deliberately slowing down your breathing, you calm your mind and body. Sometimes, I would sit on the beach, especially if it was warm and sunny, and breathe *slowly*.

People say how important sleeping well, eating well and exercising is. This is all true but can be hard when you're in the nucleus of a trauma. I found it helpful to take baby steps. I asked myself, what is *one* thing I can do today that will be good for me?

Now that I'm in a safe and happy place, I can look at my 'patchwork life' with a level of objectivity and appreciate the many lessons I gained from my journey. I have learnt that if you have a positive attitude and are grateful for the small things around you, your world *does* change. You attract what you focus on, so if you focus on the good around you and are thankful for it, more of it will come.

Educating yourself in personal development is empowering, and it is *never* too late to learn or change.

Dwelling on trivial things, or things you can't change is a waste of energy.

Being critical of myself is not helpful. Being kind and loving towards myself is helpful.

Family doesn't just mean the people you share DNA with. You can choose your family by finding other people who you love and love you.

Despite how you may feel, you are never alone. There is plenty of love in the world for everyone.

Intuition can be a powerful guide if we tune into it. I ignored my intuition for far too long.

If you are where I have been, please trust that you can rise from the lowest of places. Look after yourself, and if you have good friends to lean on, then do that. If you don't, then use the services that are available for whatever you need. There are many kind people in social welfare, and if you happen to encounter someone who doesn't care, don't take it personally. Just persist until you find the good people. If I can turn my life around from where I was to where I am now, so can you. And you deserve it.

Chapter 19

My New York Way

Pip Rae

Rising from PTSD.

'I use my strengths in the arena they are meant for and create a flow that feels good, does good and brings joy.'

Law and Order was one of my favourite TV programs. Maybe I watched one too many episodes, but whatever the reason, I entered the police force as a teenager with one ambition: to make the world a better place.

With a healthy lifestyle and promising career, I was beaming with vitality and optimism. I swam in the ocean, loved socialising, sewing, travelling, and helping people. Life, outside of my work, was fun.

Police officers are exposed to a plethora of traumas in their work that, to most people, would stand out among the worst in their lives. From abused children, dead bodies, severe assaults, sex crimes, riots, shootings, homes broken into, families torn apart, to carnage on the road and domestic violence, we see it all. Regardless of the training we are given to handle it, the traumas accumulate over time, and in my case, they distorted my reality and etched away at my sense of safety.

It's the daily work that creates an invisible burden police officers carry with them everywhere. After four years of service, every shift felt like 1000 cuts scratching the top layer of my skin. It would hurt for a while then heal, but the following day, the scar would be reopened by the calls for assistance and the investigations of crime.

It was not the world, but me who changed.

After about ten years, I was medicating myself with alcohol, food and distracting myself by being too busy. On the outside, I looked like an overachiever, pleasing, doing and being everything to everybody, except myself. I welcomed therapy and dived headfirst into art therapies and creativity. They were fun, but they didn't help my mental health.

Trapped inside a distorted reality, I was diagnosed with

chronic post-traumatic stress disorder (PTSD) – a mental health condition that results from long-term exposure to trauma, which occurs during times of extreme vulnerability, and more often involving power imbalances.

Agitated, frustrated and intolerant, my language became harsh and hostile. I would disassociate and keep others at arm's length to protect that vulnerability and hide the shame of not coping. My personal relationships fractured, and my confidence was smashed. I constantly sought reassurance and gathered evidence to prove the world was a bad place, and that I needed to stay on alert.

Gone was the young extrovert. Gone was my fit body and healthy self. Gone were my hobbies.

I'd stay up late, not wanting to sleep, fearing the nightmares would return. Being constantly tired, I became sensitive and highly reactive to noises. Sirens, screams and the screech of a car breaking would trigger me. I'd hold my breath waiting for the sound of the crash. I avoided public places, transport, and people who I perceived to be threatening. Driven by fear, and constantly hyper-vigilant, I would cross to the other side of the road if someone was following behind me on a footpath. I sat with my back to the front door of a café, drove home a different way each day and was reactive to feedback and criticism.

By this stage, I'd been medically discharged from the police force and was in what they called 'recovery'. Coinciding with this, was the irretrievable breakdown of my marriage. Although it was an unhealthy relationship, I was terrified of being on my own. With small children, no job or career prospects, being miserable didn't feel as bad as the alternative.

However, with the help of a counsellor, I realised an important lesson. What we allow and enable in relationships teaches people how to treat us. If we allow anything less than respect, our self-worth eventually erodes. I used to justify my difficult relationship with my husband by telling myself that I had seen much worse. Eventually, however, it became intolerable, and although it was traumatic at the time, the cutting of ties became liberating.

Although my identity was shattered into a thousand shards, this personal 'disaster' became an opportunity to pick up the pieces of shard I wanted to keep and let go of everything else. It became an opportunity to create a better life. As I journalled my way through this process, I reached out to a friend who helped me reframe my story from 'victim' to 'victor'.

I embraced the resilience skills that I used in work situations and applied them to my personal chaos. I reminded myself that everything is 'figure-out-able'. With a calm mind, everything is solvable. Emotional regulation work with a Somatic Trauma therapist helped restore my calmness, confidence and faith that I would be ok.

I changed my lifestyle to create the person I wanted to become. I switched from using alcohol to numb the pain to organic food, exercise and meaningful conversations with wise and empathetic people. With restored, positive energy, I attracted new people in my life. I made new female friends, set boundaries, painted for pleasure, swam, and travelled, despite my fears. It was this matrix of techniques, tools and mindset that helped me create an identity that I began to recognise and love. I was re-uniting with my old, authentic self.

Step by tiny step, I replaced the missing shards of unworthiness with healthier ones such as gratitude and kindness. I learnt how to validate myself and remove the need to pursue acceptance or permission from others. I learnt how the art of detachment from people or dramas opens the door to freedom and a world of new possibilities.

On my road to recovery, there were obstacles and potholes – mainly in the form of some people who resisted my change. Consequently, I packed up my fears and said goodbye to victimhood, and to my married life in Sydney.

On the 24 November 2017, my three children and I headed to New York City for a month of transition from housewife and homemaker to … well … whatever I wanted to be. As Shannon L. Alder wrote: 'Every woman that finally figured out her worth, has picked up her suitcases of pride and boarded a flight to freedom, which landed in the valley of change.'

We arrived on Thanksgiving with three priorities – fun, independence and kindness.

Each morning, I walked to Central Park while the kids slept in, and I returned home with a hearty breakfast for us all to enjoy. On my walk, I loved watching the people run around the lake or sit reading the paper – I was fascinated with how they did life! I journalled feelings, set intentions for the day, and I simply sat and rested. Within days, I became lighter in my thoughts, thinner around my waist, calmer in my mind and stronger in my spirit.

A week passed by, and my 16-year-old son said, 'You seem different.' It made me realise that I *was* different. I created that change by taking charge of my life, eliminating what I didn't want and going after what I wanted. After all, we're not ornaments. We're not *meant* to stay the same. We're breathing, beating, ever-evolving humans – being.

For me, New York City was full of lessons and metaphors. As I stood on the footpath of a library in midtown, I stared at the detail of the statues – *Patience* and *Fortitude* – two sitting lions that guard the millions of pieces of knowledge and wisdom preserved within the heritage walls. The names were given to the lions by Mayor Fiorello La Guardia, who felt New Yorkers needed these virtues to get through the Great Depression.

A quick subway ride to Wall Street and I stared admiringly at the feminine strength of the young girl facing down the raging bull. My children and I continued to wander downtown. After climbing the steps to the entrance of the Supreme Court, we sat and I quietly pondered the injustice of the violence perpetrated against women. Until that moment, I had considered it a social reality that I was powerless to change. *But then again*, I thought, *maybe I could?*

We meandered to the Museum of the City of New York where a new exhibition called 'Beyond Suffrage, A Century of New York Women in Politics' had started. Momentum for social change had been building since 16 October, when American actress Alyssa Milano posted on Twitter, 'If all the women who have been sexually harassed or assaulted wrote 'Me too' as a status, we might give people a sense of the magnitude of the problem.' As the ground swell of collective grief was palpable, I 'accidentally' found myself in the thick of #MeToo.

The prevalence of sexual violence and sexual coercion was estimated to affect one-third of all women worldwide, but it was the publication of a poll in *The Washington Post* that reported 54% percent of American women report receiving 'unwanted and inappropriate' sexual advances, with 95 percent saying that such behaviour usually goes unpunished. These statistics startled me, and the stories of sexual abuse continued to unveil each day across all platforms of media.

Many factors – my life experience, the problems of systematic failures, community attitudes, the impact of abuse, *where* I was and *when* I was there – collectively conspired to lead me to my new-found purpose. New York reminded me that while we don't get to choose the start of our life story, we *do* get to choose how our story evolves.

It was then time to fly home and begin a new chapter. Better still, I would begin an exciting new novel!

The kids and I spent Christmas Day crossing the Atlantic Ocean in the air. As I walked out of the sliding glass doors of the airport, I saw my reflection of the new me. A version I had been desperate to find and reclaim stared back at me. She was the strong, independent and courageous girl who wanted to be the change she wished to see in the world. I smiled at her with a glow of pride.

Creating a new life after divorce and Chronic PTSD hasn't been without struggles and fear, but with purpose, courage, gratitude, patience and fortitude, I now feel I can cope with any situation life throws at me. I'm independent and use my strengths in the arena they are meant for and create a flow that feels good, does good and brings joy.

The current systems and processes are not fit for purpose in protecting victims, and their voices are silenced and overshadowed by victim blaming and excuses. I show up in the state I want others to be in and thrive in my new role as an advocate and private investigator for domestic violence victims. I help victims create a strategy to leave an abusive relationship while building their confidence and self-worth.

In 2021, my work for women's protection was acknowledged with various accolades, including: the Australian Women in Security Network award; the Peacemaker for Diversity award; and the AusMumprenuer Women's Champion award. While I appreciate these acknowledgements, the greatest reward for me is seeing women transform from their life of fear and misery to empowerment.

When counselling victims of domestic violence, I offer the following advice:

- Measure success on your terms, not by the opinions of others.
- Let go of the past. Rebuild a life that focuses on your values and emulates the people you admire.
- Choose your language carefully. Try articulating what you are *experiencing,* instead of labelling yourself. For example, instead of 'I am a *victim* of domestic violence …', say 'I am *subjected to* domestic violence' or, 'I am *disempowered by* controlling behaviours ….' Words are loaded with power, so try to avoid disempowering words.
- Know your boundaries and enforce them.
- Adversity is an opportunity to grow self-awareness. So, be honest about the role you play in conflict or harm.
- Learn to love your authentic self and walk into any arena with your head held high.
- Trust your intuition.
- Unlearn old beliefs that cause you harm, and replace them with healthy new beliefs.
- Sleep is important. Learn and practise good sleeping habits.

- Be of service to others through volunteering or advocating for change. Being kind helps others *and* you feel better.
- Be kind to yourself and give yourself permission to laugh and have fun.
- Find and invest in *quality* friends who support your journey.
- Have a bucket of strategies and use whichever you need at the time. If you don't know which to use, ask for help.
- Find quotes that lift you, and display them in places you often see. One of my favourites is:

  '*Anything that annoys you is teaching you patience.*

  Anyone who abandons you is teaching you how to stand on your own two feet.

  Anything that angers you is teaching you forgiveness and compassion.

  Anything that has power over you is teaching you to how take your power back.

  Anything you hate is teaching you unconditional love.

  Anything you fear is teaching you courage to overcome your fear.

  Anything you can't control is teaching you how to let go.

  Everything in life is teaching you something.'

  Luke Chlebowicz

Remember that you are the author of your own story. You get to write the next chapter, or perhaps a wonderful novel.

Photo by Emma Phillips

Chapter 20

The Justice Warrior

Margaret Cunneen, SC

Rising from wrongful corruption charges.

'My sons reminded me to face the world as a warrior. They encouraged me to fight.'

By 2014, at the age of 55, I had reached a level of achievement in my legal career of which I was proud. I had started out, at just 18, as a clerk in the New South Wales Attorney General's Department. I worked my way up, while also studying bachelor's and master's degrees in law. For decades, I worked enormously hard as a Crown Prosecutor, invariably in the prosecution of crimes of personal violence – murder, sexual assault of children and adults, and serious personal assaults.

I had the experience of abuse at a very young age and felt for many years after that I had no voice. I knew that children, and indeed most victims of assault, had limited credibility in the courts. I started prosecuting child sexual assault in the mid-1980s and wanted to make the court experience an easier one for abused children, some of whom were doubted even by their own parents.

If there was any criticism of me, it was for 'getting too close' to the victims of crime with whom I worked to obtain justice in their cases. That came, of course, from lawyers who worked on the opposite end of the Bar table. For the victims, and, in murder cases, the bereaved relatives of the victims, giving evidence in serious criminal trials was the most difficult time of their lives. As the mother of three adult children, it was only natural that I would be warm and encouraging in any way I could to support these people. I had always taken my role as a public servant quite literally. I was there to do everything I could to assist the public, whose taxes paid my wages.

It was gratifying to have received numerous messages of thanks over the years. I often felt that my counselling side was perhaps of more assistance than my legal side.

Chapter 20

By mid-2014, I had just completed a Special Commission of Inquiry into the historical cases of paedophile priests in the Maitland-Newcastle area. My report, which I had personally delivered to the Governor, had been well-received, particularly by the many victims of child sexual abuse from the region.

I was told of rumours that I was to be appointed a Supreme Court judge. I wouldn't have accepted the appointment; however, just as I had declined an appointment to the District Court seven years before. I loved being a barrister, assisting people closely and directly with the dreadful circumstances of their appearances in courts. I didn't want to be a 'referee'.

On the last day of my appointment as Commissioner of the Inquiry, my eldest son's girlfriend, Sophia, then 24, was injured in a car crash. She was stationary at traffic lights when another car crashed directly into her driver's door. Her car was crushed and turned on its side, and she was suspended by the seatbelt. Sophia was rescued from the wreck by bystanders, and her phone and possessions were left in the car. When the ambulance arrived, before the attendance of any police, Sophia was placed in the rear and transported to hospital with severe pain to her chest and ribs. Upon arrival, routine blood tests were taken, which recorded 0.00% alcohol and no drugs. This was never a surprise to any of us, as she was returning alone in the car from work, on a normal afternoon. The other driver was charged with dangerous driving.

The crisis that befell our family arose from the innocuous fact that Sophia was driving a car that I, as part of my salary package, had leased from my employer, the Office of the Director of Public Prosecutions. It was perfectly acceptable for me, under the rules, to use this car in a private capacity, and so I lent it to Sophia on this day. As it turned out, there were people employed in secretive investigation agencies who did not understand this.

The catalyst was the fact that a tow truck driver who attended the crash, and who, much later, handed his phone to a smash repairer to talk to me, was being intercepted by an investigation agency. When my son, Steve, and I were summoned to the crash by friends who witnessed it (it was not far from our home), Sophia had already been taken from the scene. The tow truck driver asked for my number and told me that he would tow the wreck to a nearby smash repairer. Sometime later, the smash repairer determined that the car couldn't be salvaged. The tow truck driver happened to be with him at the time and rang my number so that the smash repairer could deliver the news.

The smash repairer asked who the registered owner was, and I told him, 'The DPP.'

He responded with a groan.

Perhaps I should have said, 'Everything's ok', as it certainly was, under the leasing conditions.

Two months later, operatives from the New South Wales Independent Commission Against Corruption (ICAC) raided my home and my son's home, which he shared with Sophia. All our phones were seized without warrants. We weren't told why, and we had absolutely no idea what they were looking for.

In fact, because the then head of the ICAC was a woman with whom I had worked closely with for many years, my immediate thought was that it was some kind of practical joke and that I should remain cool. I did, but I told them it was illegal to storm my home and seize my property without a warrant.

A week later, without warning, the seizures were re-enacted, this time *with* warrants. Yes, they brought the phones back and put them down on a table. I thought they were being returned! A minute later, they picked them up again, filming the lot.

Nothing happened for the following three months, except that I was asked by telephone 'from ICAC' to supply my 'government e-tag (electronic toll device) records for the car Sophia was driving'. I told the caller that I had never had a government e-tag and that the one installed in the car was my own. *Why did they want my e-tag records?* The 'investigator' said he wanted to check what time the car had crossed the Sydney Harbour Bridge.

'Well, that won't help,' I said. 'There is no toll going north.'

The caller was quiet for a minute, but they insisted on wanting the records anyway.

On the early morning of Halloween, which was a fitting metaphor of this witch-hunt fiasco, there were numerous media cameras outside my home. I wasn't aware until my middle son, Matt, turned and ran back down the side passage where I was saying goodbye to him in my dressing gown. By this stage, I had been ordered to go on leave by the head of the DPP because I was the subject of an ICAC investigation. This was despite the fact it was clear the matter had nothing to do with the course of my duties, but about someone else's car crash. That day, and many, many days after that, I was all over the news.

The allegation that emerged was that I had told Sophia to 'fake chest pain' so that she could avoid a police breath test. Allegedly, I somehow conveyed this advice through my son Steve (no doubt because there were no phone calls whatsoever between Sophia and me) and that Sophia had done as I had told her. All three of us were accused by ICAC of 'perverting the course of justice'.

The allegation was totally misconceived from the start. I have ever since been grateful to the then Commissioner of Police, who, the day the news broke, released a statement saying that Sophia had undergone a blood test immediately after she arrived at the hospital, which was negative, and there was no wrongdoing by any member of my family.

Moreover, the other driver announced that he was the one who was at fault.

ICAC didn't ever interview any witnesses at the scene. Later, however, they were interviewed by *The Australian* newspaper and affirmed that there could never have been the prospect of a police breath test, as Sophia had been taken by ambulance before the police arrived. The bystanders who rescued Sophia from the wreck didn't detect any trace of alcohol. They stayed with her, of course, and verified that there was no opportunity for me to give or send any message to her, directly or otherwise.

Despite this information, ICAC announced a full-blown inquiry to investigate not just me, but Sophia and Steve as well. We wouldn't have the benefit of the rules of evidence or the right to silence, as we would if answering a criminal charge in a proper court.

If it had only been me in the crosshairs of this bumbling, but enormously powerful organisation, I would have fronted up and tried to explain where they had got it wrong. I would have done the 'walk of shame' that ICAC, in that era, orchestrated. The process was the punishment, regardless of the eventual outcome down the track.

However, my protective motherhood instinct compelled me to be strong for Steve and Sophia. When they asked me what their summonses were all about, I explained that the ICAC just wanted me. After all, as a public official, I was the only one of us who should have been under their eye. I told them they didn't have to worry and resolved to save my family from being humiliated, bullied, publicly shamed and, ultimately, very probably imprisoned. With me. Because of me.

With enduring faith, I prayed for strength and justice – and I initiated proceedings in the proper courts to establish that ICAC had no jurisdiction to investigate an allegation that, even if it were true, had nothing to do with corruption.

During the experience, I discovered who my true friends were – the ones who believed in me instantly and encouraged and supported me all the way. Some close friends (now not so much), thought I had done something wrong and said that it was no use trying to stop it – it would go ahead. Some people who I had known for years plainly snubbed me. Later, some of them were to say, 'I wanted to call you, but your phone was probably tapped.'

I would reply, 'So, you thought you'd be in trouble for being a loyal friend?'

Others who stopped calling would contact me years later with no reference to the hugely public ordeal my family had endured, and then proceed to ask me for legal advice or some other favour. I would ask, 'Have you been out of the country for the last few years?'

Even though we were to win our legal case against ICAC, their appeal (which we also won), dragged the matter out further. Even after that, the ICAC, who had trawled through nine years of my text messages, kept trying to harm me by sending some of the messages to my employer, alleging breaches of an employment code of conduct. Once again, they had the wrong end of the stick.

Underlying this whole debacle was a personal animosity that became a trenchant stubbornness driving this on. Despite my family and me being fully exonerated, the residual taint of the attack meant that there was no offer of any judicial appointment, not that I cared.

Early in the two-year battle, which kept changing form, I took up the sport of boxing. It is a great form of exercise at any age. I still train at least twice a week eight years later. Physical exercise is extremely important when facing any difficulty in life. Working out releases endorphins that make you feel better about everything. Exercise helps to put things in perspective. I had the joy of training with my three sons, who are all accomplished martial artists. My sons reminded me to face the world as a warrior. They encouraged me to fight. My boys and their dad enveloped me with their courage and strength.

'Who cares what they think, Mum? We're with you.'

I fought hard and publicly disseminated the truth of Sophia's crash through speeches, newspaper articles, radio and television appearances. Eventually, the message that ICAC had gone rogue gained momentum, and the Courts, the Crown Solicitor and the ICAC Inspector declared the investigation misconceived and should never have commenced.

I returned to work as a Crown Prosecutor and retired from the role when it suited me, at sixty.

I am now a busy criminal defence barrister. The change of perspective, and the stimulation of working for myself after

42 years in the public service, makes me feel like I am fresh out of school! It marked a new beginning, surrounded by people who admire me rather than sneer at me. The ICAC ordeal put me on the map as someone who fought like crazy for justice for her family and herself. I know how it feels to be falsely accused, and this empathy has been very good for my clients and business.

Working for myself has also given me with time to write a book – *The Boxing Butterfly* – which is a memoir of my career in prosecuting murderers, paedophiles and rapists; turning the tables on ICAC; and my new chapter as a defence barrister.

My family and I have reaped other rewards from our struggle. We became more cohesive and grew in wisdom, loyalty and love. Our resilience was tested and strengthened because of our journey.

I can distil my resilience tools into 'four Fs': my family, friends, fitness and faith in God. All these factors, collectively, gave me strength and perspective.

When counselling my clients through their ordeals, I tell them that at my age I have seen that everyone, at some time in their lives, suffers a major tragedy or humiliation or otherwise horrendous event. I am usually able to reassure young adults that this is that ordeal in their lives. They are lucky to be getting their major battle of life behind them when they are young. I encourage them to be strong and remind them that it will pass.

I have been fascinated to find that every client I have had since I came to private practice, whether Sikh, Muslim, Christian, Jewish, Pacific Islander or even Chinese, has been delighted, and even keen, to pray with me. Faith in God, for people in deep trouble, is the ultimate tool of resilience.

Chapter 21

Master of Disaster

Sandra Black

Rising from a catastrophic cyclone.

'It's true that there are always gifts in adversity, and Cyclone Debbie is no exception.'

There is something about disasters that has always attracted me. Not causing them but preparing for them and fixing the mess afterwards. Maybe it's my strong protective instinct, or maybe it's my genuine care for people and our environment. Whatever the reason, while I worked in the finance department for the Whitsunday Regional Council, I was always looking sideways at the disaster department, and I volunteered in the Disaster Coordination Centre for 16 years.

As a single mum of my nine-year-old daughter, Harriet, I had a balanced, happy life with four areas of focus – Harriet, work, study (of Public Safety) and my gardening. My house had a high fence, so I always felt safe and private while I gardened. It was my happy place where I enjoyed creating beauty, getting my hands dirty and rejuvenating from life's daily pressures.

In 2016, I was offered a position for one day a week in the Disaster Management Unit as the Local Recovery Coordinator. I was so excited, as I knew it opened the door to advance my skills and do what I love – managing disasters. In my job interview, I had even said that I wanted to be 'a master of disaster'. Shortly after undertaking the new role, my skills and ambition were sorely tested.

One of my first tasks was to update Council's official Disaster Management Recovery Plans and ensure our Recovery groups were formalised. Like me, it was tidy, shiny and promising, but untested.

Six months into my new position, information from the Bureau of Meteorology (BOM) was formidable. Tropical Cyclone Debbie, with wind speeds up to 263 kilometres, was on her way. It was time to implement the Disaster

Management Plan, a part of which was setting up a Local Disaster Coordination Centre. With a sense of foreboding, I also organised my family (Harriet and my sister's family) to be in a safe house *together*. I cooked ten litres of spaghetti bolognaise for the coordination centre, then returned to duty.

As the cyclone moved down from the north, intensifying her strength, we orchestrated the mobilisation of hundreds of emergency workers to prepare. With the cyclone potentially merging with high tide, a major storm surge was threatening. We moved from voluntary evacuation to mandatory evacuation orders, in symphony with a myriad of agencies – police, maritime safety, ambulance, fire and rescue, and many more.

In the state of Queensland, more than 400 schools, airports, harbours, and train services were closed and 25,000 people evacuated their homes and boats. Many people filled the evacuation centres across the state. Despite orders, some people in the Whitsundays refused to leave their homes or get off their boats, which was stressful and frustrating in the circumstances.

On 28 March 2017, Cyclone Debbie struck the Whitsundays with the fury of Category 4 winds and torrential rains. I went to work at the Coordination Centre early that morning and didn't return until three days later. In the midst of the storm, there was a lot of noise from the wind and the banging of tin sheets on the roof. What began as a small dripping leak in the mayor's office became a torrent of water and finally a collapsed roof. We were soon wading around in water in our office shoes while emergency electricians, who arrived to help, were wearing gumboots! This difference was disturbing. A hole was drilled in the floor to drain the water, and we carried on working in a building that would soon be condemned.

During those critical three days of the before, during and after the storm, there was tensely fractured and fluctuating leadership in the ranks. However, overall, the staff, volunteers and emergency workers who were deployed were incredible in their care for each other and the hundreds of displaced people. As day one and two rolled into day three with barely a wink of sleep, some of us were 'drunk' from exhaustion.

Although we took our roles very seriously, at times we found ourselves giggling at the silliest of things. Comradeship and humour often kept us functioning.

When I finally returned home to my family on day three, they were celebrating the passing of Debbie. At that stage, I was beyond cheer. Instead, I collapsed in my bedroom and had a long, overdue cry and sleep.

Debbie became one of Australia's most deadly and costly cyclones. Damage extended all the way down the coast to New South Wales, due to heavy rain that followed the windstorm. In total, Debbie caused approximately $3.5 billion in damage and 14 deaths. Our local tropical paradise towns, such as Airlie Beach, and our local food bowl areas, such as Proserpine and Bowen, and the mining town of Collinsville were badly damaged and without power or water for days, even weeks in some areas. Many of our beautiful islands, particularly Hamilton, Daydream, Hayman, and Long Island, were annihilated. In one day, our beautiful, lush-green landscapes were stripped back to what resembled bush-fire scenes.

While it took about two weeks to respond to the cyclone, it took three years of intense work to recover damaged communities in our region. By intense work, I mean long working days, seven days a week. If I wasn't in the office helping to coordinate the massive recovery effort with more than a dozen agencies, I was out in the field, engaging with communities, carrying out welfare checks and meeting with stakeholders.

This took a toll on my personal life, particularly on my relationship with Harriet. Sadly, due to my lack of home time, we drifted apart. On weekends, I'd sometimes coax her out to hand out recovery and disaster information pamphlets with me, just to be with her. Why would a young teenager want to spend her weekends handing out pamphlets? Torn between my commitment to my community and my daughter, I became wracked with guilt. Not an 'oops, I dropped a glass guilt', but a deep, heartbreaking 'I'm not enough' guilt.

My energy and zest for life was slowly fading. Before Debbie, I had the sanctuary of my screened garden to heal and rejuvenate. Unfortunately, when Cyclone Debbie took my fence away, she also took my sanctuary away. My family, who I love very much, were nearby, but I wasn't inclined to openly share my feelings with them.

In 2020, I became the Disaster Management Coordinator for the council and, while I knew how to heal a broken region, I needed to heal myself.

I found the support of my colleagues, internal and external, to be immensely strengthening. I remember a few of them calling me every week to check my welfare. Each time our phone calls finished, I felt better. A mentor and friend would call me periodically and ask me, 'Sandra, have you told yourself that you're wonderful today?' Although it sounds like a cliché, being asked if you're ok really does make a difference.

Professional intervention was another key to my recovery. During a Red Cross 'Support the Supporter' program, my self-awareness grew, and I realised that I didn't look after myself. In the habit of putting everyone else first, I needed to shift my mindset and start caring for myself.

With my new self-care attitude, I took six weeks off work in 2021 to rest, enjoy myself and heal the rift between Harriet and me. This gave Harriet and I much needed one-on-one time to reconnect, and it did mend our relationship.

Writing was another tool in my personal recovery. It wasn't exactly a personal journal, but through writing a 'Transition from Recovery to Business-as-Usual' report for the council, I could appreciate how far we had come and how much we had achieved. While I was already so proud and close to my team and colleagues, the report compounded my respect and appreciation of them.

Since the onset of the disaster, my colleagues showed up every day with compassion to help our community and rebuild our region, under difficult conditions. With the loss of our council building, staff members were moved around to eight different buildings in the area. I'm blessed to work among such compassionate and adaptable people.

It's true that there are always gifts in adversity, and Cyclone Debbie is no exception. Three years on, we have beautiful, modern council offices that are far better than the original. United by our shared memories and challenges, my colleagues and I have a strong sense of comradery and loyalty at work, similar to a family bond. Without Debbie, I would not have grown so much personally, or professionally. Debbie gave me a chance to test my skills and character. It enabled me to develop grit and resilience.

Debbie also elevated my leadership skills with more clarity in how I like to work with people. I like to empower people with whatever resources they need to achieve their goals, then give them space to shine. It hasn't been an easy journey, but through Debbie, I've 'earnt' where I am today and am thankful for that.

In May 2022, I celebrated my 50th birthday and married myself. Yes, you 'heard' correctly. I married myself. It's called 'sologomy' – a commitment of love to oneself. It doesn't mean loving oneself exclusively but loving and being kind to that inner self – who is often so quiet and easy to forget – *while* loving others. Like other weddings, I wrote vows, wore a wedding dress, had bridesmaids, family, and friends … and had a ball!

My Vows

To comfort myself during times of hopelessness, despair, depression, disillusionment, or any difficulty that arises.

To be my beloved always and in all ways.

To never settle or abandon myself in romantic partnerships again.

To live in the faith that my life unfolds in mysterious divine perfection.

To honour my spiritual path and create an amazing life, whether I am ever legally married or not.

To honour my calling and live my life as a work of art.

Since then, every day has been a great day. That doesn't mean that everything is ideal, but *regardless* of what happens, I know that I'll be ok.

My father is currently in an aged-care home with dementia, and I live at home with my mother and Harriet. It's a three-way, symbiotic relationship with all of us supporting and appreciating each other. As for my garden sanctuary, our new home has high fences, and I have resumed my garden therapy.

When challenges or disasters strike your life, my advice is to not be frightened of them. Instead, learn from them, grow from them and look for the gifts that come with them. Be kind, adaptable and stay connected with others for your sake and theirs. Above all, remember *you*, take good care of *you* and love *you*.

Chapter 22

A Fall to Grace

Linda Stanley

Rising, after being told I never would.

'Recovery was not going to be served to me on a platter. It was up to me to achieve as much as I possibly could.'

My love of plants and nature came from my mother. Mum had a shadehouse and was forever taking cuttings and growing things to give away to friends and family. If I ever wanted to find Mum, I'd go to her shadehouse and find her caring for and talking to her 'flora babies'.

It was therefore only natural for me to love plants, talk to my own 'flora babies', and later, with my husband John, establish a plant nursery consultancy business. With our successful business, good health, four lovely capable daughters, a comfortable home overlooking a national park in a wonderful community in Western Australia, my life was blessed.

Our house, which was situated on a steep hillside, had a front deck that jutted over and high above a granite outcrop. In 2002, we employed a builder to replace our front deck for a party we had planned for my 50th birthday celebration. A week before the party, he suggested that we paint the battens before he put the iron on the roof. The suggestion made good sense. Our painting job would be easier without the roof, so we all agreed.

John and my 14-year-old daughter, Lara, were on a scaffold painting the battens, and I was on a ladder painting the highest point of the battens. Suddenly, my ladder wobbled then gave way. I knew it was bad and, in my mind's eye, I could see that I was heading over the edge of the deck onto the granite boulders far below. I wouldn't survive such a fall. Instinctively, I twisted myself to land on the deck. Upon impact, my vertebrae exploded.

I saved my life … but broke my back.

The following hours are hazy – a panicking family, muffled conversations, an ambulance and eventually waking up in the hospital's emergency department. John was particularly distressed, so I began assessing myself in hope of finding some good news to soothe him.

I wriggled my toes – and could feel them! 'John, I can wriggle my toes, so I'm not paralysed. My spine's not damaged!' I announced.

John, however, wasn't soothed by that at all, so I moved my hands around. 'See, it's all good, no damage.'

He still didn't seem to cheer up, and I was still wriggling my feet when a doctor came rushing into the room. 'Stop that! Don't move your legs!' he shouted. 'Please stop moving! Your vertebrae has exploded! There are fragments of bone!'

John's stress level now clearly soared to the roof, and I kept still.

A few weeks had passed when a specialist entered my room. I didn't like him at all, his manner nor his choice of words. When I asked him for my long-term prognosis, he glibly replied, 'Oh, you'll probably never walk again.' My mind numbed, and I didn't hear what came afterwards.

After he left and the shock of his words began to sink in, my dislike of him inflamed into anger. I thought, *He shouldn't say things like that to people. Some people may believe him, and just give up!* I refused to accept his prognosis and, while I was determined that his opinion wouldn't seal my fate, I sympathised with other people whose hope would be destroyed by such news. I was angry that a modern medical specialist, who would be aware of the power of our mind in healing *and* sickness, would utter such words.

As I laid that night in my hospital bed, I thought about walking again and the many obstacles ahead of me. I then had a vision that is as clear today as it was 22 years ago. There was an enormous mountain in front of me that I *had* to climb. Mentally, I threw a pick high up to the mountainside and pulled myself up. I *saw* it, then I *said* it to the universe. 'I am going to backpack around the world!'

In my mind, *this* was my future.

At that point, I realised that my recovery would be as much a mental challenge as a physical challenge. I knew I had to stay positive and, like my grandad said, 'focus'.

A few days later when John and our youngest daughter visited me in hospital, I had a hallucination that traumatised my poor husband even more. John is British and grew up in Birmingham. When we married, we lived in England for three years before we moved to my home country of Australia. In the middle of a conversation, I suddenly saw in my mind's eye that we were at the edge of a pier, in Birmingham, and I wanted to take a dip! 'John, would you climb down that ladder please and see if the water is warm enough for a dip?' I asked him.

'Where do you think we are?' John asked.

'On the pier, darling,' I replied.

'Where's the pier?' he asked.

'In Birmingham!' I was getting frustrated by his questions, and the look of shock on his face turned into one of horror.

'Do you know where Birmingham is?' he asked.

At that moment, my 'trip in my mind' was over. 'Oh!' I said. 'I'm back. I must have tripped out.'

John didn't understand. 'Do you know where Birmingham is?' he repeated.

'Yes, it's in England. But I'm back now.'

Poor John. He couldn't cope and ended up taking our daughter home. We later concluded it was the morphine.

Chapter 22

I remained in hospital for four excruciating and heavily sedated months, but fortunately, there were no more 'trips'.

I eventually returned home wearing a metal brace and was bedridden for the following 12 months. My first venture to the toilet was walking with the assistance of Lara. Inside the toilet, I then had an even bigger problem. I couldn't bend to wipe my bottom. After several minutes, Lara asked through the door if I was all right.

'No!' I answered, and she burst into the room. 'I can't wipe my bottom!'

Horror at the realisation washed over Lara. 'No! No way, Mum!'

'I did it for you as an infant.' I grinned.

'Hang on, I'll find something.' And she ran off towards the kitchen and returned with a long-handled kitchen sponge. 'Here, try this,' she suggested as she thrust it at me. It worked and saved us both from major embarrassment. We quickly learnt that laughter is a wonderful medicine.

My recovery began by finding natural ways to ease my incessant pain. Although I have an aversion to needles, I gave acupuncture a go, and to my astonishment, three visits later, my crooked spine was straightened! My doctor even told me to keep doing whatever I was doing because it was working!

I combined acupuncture with Reiki, Bowen Therapy, and Kinesiology for the next two years, and each one eased the pain a little. With the natural therapies, daily physiotherapy, and assistance to walk, I was making progress towards my goal, albeit tiny progress.

It was three years after the accident that I took my first steps aided only by an elastic brace. I felt terribly insecure and unsupported, and quite frightened, but also excited to be recovering. I later progressed to driving a car and found an old Mercedes with a comfortable seat. I felt like I was sitting on a cloud.

Just as I had inherited my love of plants from my mother, I inherited my interest in spirituality from her side of the family. Mum would explain what she called my 'second sight'. Because I was the seventh child, she would say, 'The seventh child of the seventh child has second sight.' And that was the end of the explanation, as far as she was concerned.

My grandfather, Mum's father, was also spiritual and a water dowser. My brother recalled that one day, Grandad took him to a well that had a bar across the top with a piece of string hanging from it. 'Just watch this,' Grandad said as he held his hand above the piece of string. The string began to spin in wide circles getting faster and faster, until he took his hand away and stopped it. Grandad said that it was all about 'focus'.

The first book that helped me understand some of these things was called *The Third Eye* by Lobsang Rampa. It was a relief to find that other people had similar experiences to my grandfather, and so I read many books and joined Theta Healing classes where I learnt to channel spirit. This means taking the mind into almost a form of meditation and receiving messages from whoever may come through in spirit.

During one class, my 'channelling partner' told me that my spiritual guide said I must do the Camino Trail next year. I had never heard of the Camino Trail.

'What's the Camino Trail?' I asked.

At that moment, another class member walked past and heard my question. 'Excuse me, did you just say, what's the Camino Trail? I have a book about it in my bag.'

I recognised in an instant that this was serendipity, a collusion of universal forces that were leading me to an important discovery – by 'accident'. The Universe was saying, 'You promised you would backpack around the world? Now is the time.'

The following 12 months were dedicated to preparing for the Camino Trail. Firstly, I educated myself about the trails. Hundreds of thousands of people walk across Europe to the Camino de Santiago every year. Originally, Christian pilgrims would make the long, sacred journey to the cathedral in Galicia's Santiago de Compostela, to reduce the punishment of their sins.

Today, people walk the Camino Trail for a myriad of reasons, from seeking a travel adventure and boosting fitness and health, to seeking a haven for personal reflection or transformation, or religious and spiritual aspirations. My motivations for walking the Camino Trail were clear. To challenge myself, mentally and physically, and to honour the promise I had made to the universe for the opportunity it gave me to walk again.

John was supportive of this 'fool thing' and encouraged me to boost my fitness and strength before I embarked on the trip. So, every day for a year, I would walk with a backpack loaded with increasing kilograms of weight and trekking poles, through the hills near our home. At first, I was slow and couldn't walk more than 30 or 40 minutes, but six months later, I was carrying 12 kilograms and walking for a couple of hours. I then realised that it was not only my strength and fitness I had grown, but also my confidence. *I might actually be able to do this fool thing!*

And I did. I walked 700 kilometres along the Camino

Francés, also called The French Way, to the holy city of Santiago de Compostela in Spain. The hardest day of my journey was when I was caught in a fierce storm on the top of the Pyrenees Mountains and broke my foot in a fall. I didn't know it was broken, so I limped, almost dragged, myself into the hostel that night.

I learnt many things on the Camino Trail, among them being the importance of taking a step back from life and looking at life with an overview. Most of us rush around like ants on a nest, and to what gain? We are better off if we take a deep breath, relax our body, let go of all stress and worry, and be present in the moment. This is the gift of *grace* that my spiritual guide on the Camino Trail showed me. I have recorded the full story of the trek in my book *Walking with Angels: Journey to Santiago.*

Looking back, there were several things that helped me to overcome my trials. Humour and laughter were imperative. The world is not all doom and gloom. There is much to be amused about. My family and friends frequently reminded me and enabled me to be silly and have fun.

Indeed, support of my family and friends was fundamental to my recovery. While I was disabled for three years, my family stepped in to do what I couldn't. Support from my family, friends and community also gave me a sense of belonging and being of value. Without these feelings of *belonging* and *value*, my recovery would have been much harder.

My confidence was another precious ally. You can endure pain if you believe you can, so I never gave up. I believed that I would overcome my disability and dogmatically refused to accept otherwise.

I also chose to view this journey as an exciting challenge.

To me, there was no point in feeling depressed about things I couldn't change. There was no point in tormenting myself with *if only I …* thoughts. Instead, I sought out ways to change the things I could control, such as my outlook and my physical strength.

I also knew that *I* would determine my outcome and the degree of my recovery. Recovery wasn't going to be served to me on a platter. It was up to me to achieve as much as I possibly could. It was up to me to adapt to my life changes and make the best of my situation.

As it was before my fall, my life is now full and rewarding. John and I continue to run our consultancy business and a wonderful organic chestnut farm south of Perth. Our daughters have all grown up, and I'm immersed in what I love – growing things. I feel a deep sense of peace and gratitude. Everything that happened to me has led me to this serenity. Admittedly, it hasn't been an easy journey, but rewarding.

Our perception of our experiences is shaped by how we choose to think. If we think a situation is dreadful, then it is dreadful for us. If we think that same situation is a blessing or a good thing, then that becomes our reality, and our life becomes brighter.

Trauma that happens to one person actually happens to the whole family, and everyone responds to it differently. Providing that a person doesn't harm themselves or others, there is no right or wrong way in how to deal with it. Healing is different for everyone.

Life is a temporary treasure. It is neither permanent nor predictable. Surround yourself with joyful people and help others who may have lost their joy to find it again. Joy is not meant to be vacuum-packed, frozen, and thawed out for special occasions. Joy is abundant. It can be found in your garden, your cooking, your cleaning, your conversations with supermarket check-out staff, in the person sitting beside you on the train or plane. Have fun wherever you may be.

At all costs, maintain hope and never give up.

Chapter 23

Standing Strong

Noelene Brown

Rising from my addiction to alcohol.

'We are never alone. There is always someone who has been where we have been, and sometimes the hardest part is reaching out for help.'

Loss has been a constant theme of my life. A life with many highs, but plenty of lows. It's been quite the ride. The losses have been relentless, like seemingly never-ending waves crashing against the shore. Sometimes the waves would push me over, and I would go under and struggle to breathe through the hurt and the heartbreak. Other times I would surrender, letting the waves wash over me, trying to hold my head above the water for just long enough to rest and gather my strength.

Throughout it all, there was something inside me that kept me going. Some little glimmer that occasionally flickered just enough for me to believe that I would be ok. I could never quite put my finger on it, but now that I am through to the other side, I know exactly what it was: courage, hope and faith.

My early childhood was happy, but tough. A typical farm existence with pet lambs, dogs, chooks, swimming in the river, cricket beside the shearing shed and getting lost in the simple fun of daydreaming on the grass. There were plenty of chores, and money was scarce. Dad worked hard day after day, while Mum somehow managed to always put food on the table and make ends meet.

Not long before I started my last year of high school, I met a boy at a local rodeo. His smile and soft gentle voice won me over, and we quickly formed a special bond that I hoped and believed would last forever. However, our relationship was tragically cut short by a car accident – and I didn't get to say goodbye. Looking back now, 40 years later, I can see that I never healed from the loss, and that by pushing down the hurt and heartbreak, I set myself up in a pattern of ineffectively dealing with the steady stream of losses that followed.

Chapter 23

Like many country girls, I left home to study in the city, and it wasn't long before I realised that if I stayed away from home, I didn't have to deal with the memories of my first love. Fast forward a few years, and I fell in love with a wonderfully kind man who taught me how to expect more of myself and introduced me to many new experiences – such as the Spring Racing Carnival, which was a great excuse to buy hats and shoes, get dressed up and drink champagne, lots of champagne. Moving to Melbourne was a huge, exciting step for me, but with every work promotion that came his way, the less he was home.

I soon found myself alone in a big city with an absent husband, no family, no support and feeling incredibly lonely. Within a few years, our marriage unravelled, not because we didn't love each other but because we no longer knew each other. It wasn't long after I lost my second love, that running away to London seemed like a good idea to deal with the heartache – again.

London was fun. For two years, I did what all good Aussies with a working holiday visa did back then. I worked hard in 'temp' jobs, explored Europe when I had money, and returned to London to work again. I partied hard because I discovered it was much easier to drink away my heartache than it was to deal with it. Alcohol became my friend, although I didn't think it was a problem at the time.

On one of my European trips, I found love again in Greece. Our holiday romance eventually blossomed into a remarkable relationship, a loving marriage, three beautiful babies and a permanent move to Ireland. And so began my next adventure of growing our little family and business. We worked hard and enjoyed the fruits of our labour.

Life was great … until October 2002, when the Irish Government put our major client into liquidation. We subsequently lost our business, home and land. Our babies were just one, two and three at the time, and with no stable roof over our heads, we fell into a period of moving from one rental house to the next trying to stay afloat financially.

A few months later, my father-in-law died, and then our dog died. All the while, I was fighting with the liquidator, negotiating with creditors, banks, and the tax department, while juggling three toddlers and a life that was falling apart at every seam. With the immense and unrelenting pressure, my mental health, self-esteem and confidence plummeted.

Eventually, I accepted that I was suffering from depression and needed help. I switched from alcohol to medication, which numbed everything – the good and the bad – and functioned at a low level, just enough to take care of my children.

There was no respite from the relentless media coverage of the biggest liquidation to hit Ireland at that time. My husband and I decided that the best course was to take the financial hit from our business personally, rather than declare bankruptcy. Not for one day have I regretted that decision, because even now I can put my head on the pillow at night knowing that everything we did back then was to look after others – family, staff and creditors. I am proud of that.

For many years, we struggled to pay off the debt, but the global financial crisis began to take its grip on Ireland, and we decided to make a fresh start in Australia. So, with three children, five suitcases and one-way tickets, we set off. I felt safe returning to home soil.

However, my husband found it difficult to settle in Australia, and within a year, our marriage was in trouble. It was an amicable separation, and we both tried hard to protect our children from the fallout, but our best intentions became unstuck. I remember clearly thinking that if I just had a drink every now and again, I could handle the trauma.

My husband desperately missed his Irish family and, when our children were teenagers, he returned to Ireland – with them. While I understood that they were going home to their family and old school friends, I didn't like it, not one bit. For me, this was the biggest heartbreak of all. As a mother, I had lost my beautiful children to the other side of the world, and I was alone – again.

Very soon, however, I found my old friend – in the form of a glass and a bottle of wine. This time around, however, I needed even more alcohol to numb my aching heart. Losing my children, on top of everything else, was just unbearable.

To the outside world, I looked as though I was coping, or so I thought. I rarely drank in public. It was always at home, by myself, behind closed doors. I spent my days planning to drink, my nights drinking, and my mornings recovering from drinking. For years it was a never-ending cycle revolving entirely around my new friend. Drinking numbed decades of buried pain.

Then a very special man came into my life and helped me to change it. He encouraged my faith in God and in myself, and he helped me to stoke that little flicker of courage and hope inside me. With his love and support, I made a promise to myself to overcome the addiction to alcohol.

At the time, I was living in the remote Kimberley region of Western Australia, so finding help wasn't easy. Burdened with so much guilt, shame and stigma about drinking, I didn't want to show up at a local meeting where people would find out. My best solution was an online program that I could do privately. Every day for three months, I diligently followed the program, learnt everything I could about alcohol as an addictive substance and treated my recovery as non-negotiable.

Empowered with scientific facts about alcohol and its effect on our mind and body, my resolve to stop drinking strengthened. It was through gaining knowledge around alcohol and how it was affecting my body, mind and emotions that I was able to finally break free from it.

I learnt that alcohol, as an addictive substance, was the problem and that while it wasn't my fault, it was *my responsibility* to do something about it. This was the game changer for me because then I was able to give myself grace and compassion for everything that I had been through, including becoming addicted to alcohol, and start the process of healing my broken life.

I took a long, hard look at *why* I was drinking and learnt effective new ways to deal with my losses and heartache without using alcohol. I developed a tool kit of resources, which included a coach, a structured program, and a group of people like me who needed to break free from the clutches of alcohol. Although this emotional resilience work was hard, it was nowhere near as hard as the life I had been living while drinking.

At the same time, I entrenched new healthy habits in my alcohol-free life: prioritising sleep, drinking lots of water and eating well. Consequently, my physical health improved, my mental health improved, I found a new sense of calm, and my relationships started to heal. I was able to rebuild my life with a renewed sense of hope for the future. I now simply choose not to drink, and that is true freedom from alcohol.

It was through my own journey to freedom from alcohol that I found a passion for helping others find support when alcohol becomes a problem. I took my knowledge and experience and trained as a certified sobriety coach. I now work with people living in rural and remote areas of Australia to help them recover and rebuild their lives without alcohol. Through online programs and one-on-one coaching, I now offer the support to others that I needed all those years ago. I understand the stigma and shame that comes with having a problematic relationship with alcohol, but also that it is much easier to quit drinking when you have a program to follow and someone to encourage and support you along the way.

Perhaps the most valuable lesson I have learnt is that we are never alone. There is always someone who has been where we have been, and sometimes the hardest part is reaching out for help. An addiction to alcohol is nothing to be ashamed of. Addiction does not discriminate.

So, life continues and the wounds from the waves of losses have healed. My children, all now young adults, have returned and I am enjoying a beautiful new life with the wonderful man who led me to my recovery. And I am fulfilling my purpose – to help others just like me who need a hand up.

So, summon your courage, reach out for help, lean into your faith and stand strong.

Chapter 24

Landed

Mia Findlay

Rising from my eating disorder.

'I never had a death wish, only a survival wish.'

I was a confident and self-assured teenager before my eating disorder began. I have special memories of boarding school – living with my friends, starring in the school plays and musicals, playing sport on the weekends with my parents cheering from the sidelines. I knew who I was and who I wanted to be. I wanted to be creative and help people in some way. I was always drawn to the 'underdog' story – the people who were forgotten or overlooked.

My happiest memories from before my eating disorder are being in nature with my dad. At the top of a trail, we would carefully select a walking stick, which was a small branch casually discarded by the gum trees, and walk for hours. Dad taught me to count the rings of a tree trunk to learn its age. He crushed eucalyptus leaves between his worn fingers and held them up for me to take in the heady scent. I felt safest and most comfortable in the wild with Dad as my teacher, guide and protector.

However, in 2006, at the age of 19, my family fell apart. My mother and stepfather found themselves in a contentious, violent and explosive divorce, and I found myself in the middle of it as a witness and mediator. My bond with Dad was also fractured, and we drifted away from each other. My sense of responsibility for my mother's marriage and the survival of our family felt impossible and essential. It all felt too much. So much so, I left university where I was in my first year studying journalism.

As the pressure built, I found myself eating less and noticed that eating less awoke a voice in my head I hadn't heard before. It was pleased with less food in my body and rewarded me with a feeling of calm and control, which I was desperately craving. But when I did eat, the voice in my head would pick up a megaphone and scream at me for being worthless, weak and useless. It told me to get rid of the food from my body. So, I did and once again, I was rewarded with calm and control.

The voice increasingly set rules for me to follow, which became so numerous and complicated, they were impossible to follow, so I tried harder to meet its demands. It told me what I could eat and when, what I couldn't eat and when I had to throw it up, how often I had to exercise and for how long, what I could wear, who I could see, how many calories, sugar and fat I could eat, and how many carbs.

The voice hated my body and pointed out all the ways it could be improved, including evidence that I should be deeply ashamed of my appearance and who I was at my core. I was not only ashamed, but I was consumed by that shame. I thought of my body 24 hours a day, seven days a week. I inspected it, punished it, hid it and hated it. I routinely woke up at two o'clock in the morning so the voice could remind me of all the rules I had to follow again when the sun came up.

And fuelled by it all was a deep knowing that if I could just follow this ever-growing list of rules, then I could be safe, worthy and loveable. I believed my life, which continued to fall apart around me, could regain some sense of control if only I could master control over my food and body. What I failed to notice was that I wasn't holding the reins of the control. An eating disorder was holding them and maintained power over me for the next six years.

I took the eating disorder with me everywhere – to my job, to my catch-ups with friends, and to London when I moved there for a year. From the outside, my life looked entirely functional. I was able to work, socialise and travel, but that was one of the rules too. I was not allowed to struggle in a visible way, as this would require help from other people and would add 'weak' and 'selfish' to the ever-growing list of my insufficiencies.

However, it became increasingly difficult to hide the concerning consequences of my routines. My hair started to fall out, my body was weak, and my period disappeared. When people close to me raised their concern, I nonchalantly waved their queries away, insisting I was fine. In fact, I was never better! But the more concerning escalation they couldn't see was the new chorus the voice was playing in my head. Not only was I worthless, but I didn't deserve to live. In fact, wouldn't everyone be better off without me?

That chorus turned from a whisper to a booming demand over the following two years. Until, at the age of 25, taking my life was all I could think about. So much so, I couldn't concentrate at work or leave my house. The functional veneer I managed for the prior six years started to fall away. I lost my job, my friends, and I stopped speaking to my family until it was just me and the voice in the cold, damp apartment I could no longer afford.

The voice didn't just have a plan for food and my body anymore. It also had a plan for how I could take myself out of the world. And on one otherwise uneventful morning, I executed that plan.

The first and most important lesson I learnt was mid-way through my suicide attempt. As I made my way towards completing the eating disorder's task, it started to get quieter. It was getting what it wanted, after all. And in that silence, I started to panic and from that panic, I became angry. *How did I get here?* It made me wonder, *do I really believe this is what I deserve?* A voice I hadn't heard since I was 19 then floated back to the surface. *This is wrong.*

And that anger compelled me to pick up the phone to call my family. For the first time in my life, I asked for help. Not just for the suicide attempt, but for everything leading up to it – the self-hatred, rules, behaviours and hopelessness. I was quickly diagnosed with anorexia binge purge subtype, depression and anxiety, and I was referred to a psychologist. I surrendered to the process and looked at all the promises my eating disorder made me (safety, control, self-acceptance, happiness, hope) and compared them to where I ended up (self-loathing, hopelessness and at risk of losing my life). They couldn't be more opposite.

My therapist helped me unpack all the reasons I'd ended up in this place. She taught me *self-compassion*, especially for the shame I held for developing an eating disorder, and for coping when nothing else showed up.

I came to understand the condition as a poorly made life raft. I'd been dropped into the ocean, with no sign of land and nothing to hold onto, until an eating disorder floated by – a badly built life raft full of holes – which I grabbed onto, as anyone at risk of drowning would. But even as it filled with water and started to plummet towards the ocean floor, I kept holding onto it.

My therapist and family helped me to let go of the dodgy life raft and onto a boat called recovery, and we headed towards the safety of land. With their help and support, I disproved my fears about food and destructive beliefs about my body. I found other ways to cope and learnt to lean on others. Understanding my eating disorder in this way was essential. I never had a death wish, only a survival wish.

I started making a video diary about what I was learning in therapy, to keep track of my progress and to refer to on tough days. I put these on YouTube when I ran out of room to store them on my computer. Suddenly, people started writing in the comment section little notes of encouragement and understanding – there were people from all over the world going through recovery.

As I recovered, I noticed something else showing up on my YouTube channel. Comments about the lack of access to treatment, poor funding for eating disorders all over the world, and tales of people who wanted desperately to get better but couldn't. I felt that anger rise again, the one I felt on the day I tried to take my life. *This is wrong.*

My videos evolved towards advocacy, highlighting the injustices in eating disorder treatment. There are a million Australians suffering from an eating disorder and only 37 public hospital beds! This disease has the *highest* mortality rate of all mental illnesses, and yet it has the *lowest* funding! It was time for change.

With tens of thousands of people following my YouTube channel – 'What Mia Did Next' – we contributed to that change. As a group of survivors, we raised money and spread our message of hope in a space of hopelessness for many.

Eventually, fully recovered, I ended up right where my 19-year-old self had hoped she would – telling stories, making change and backing the underdog.

I would never wish an eating disorder on anyone, and I feel extraordinarily fortunate to have experienced the process of recovery through which I learnt so much about myself – my patterns, experiences and beliefs – which I was previously unaware of.

I learnt the importance of making sure I am ok first and foremost, before rushing to anyone else's rescue, for we can't show up for anyone else unless we are showing up for ourselves.

I learnt that the eating disorder was not a malevolent force. It was a spokesperson for the most vulnerable, hurt part of me. This understanding taught me to never shame the darker, more complex parts of myself, but to listen to what they are trying to tell me.

I learnt that I am not alone. I was encouraged online from afar by a community of incredible people who were in the recovery fight with me. And I was cheered on by those closest to me from the side lines. We are not meant to walk any path alone. We are just like any other herd animal and need each other.

And above all, I learnt that vulnerability isn't weakness. My vulnerability created a community of over 80,000 people. It allows me to speak on behalf of The Butterfly Foundation as their ambassador to eradicate the stigma surrounding eating disorders, and it has given me purposeful work as an accredited eating disorder recovery coach in my own business – Beyond Body Coaching.

My life is now calm and purposeful, and I appreciate every moment. Whether I'm at a friend's wedding, or on a plane heading to an adventure, or watching a kangaroo hop across my path in the bush, I am struck by the question, *what if I wasn't here for this?*

I am determined to make that a reality for as many people as possible. Whether through my advocacy or coaching role, it is my mission to ensure that we save as many people as we can from this deadly illness.

My safest and happiest place is still in the bush, with a walking stick in hand, counting tree trunk rings. But now I walk it alone, having lost my dad to cancer in 2019. I pretend he is just out of sight on the path ahead of me, still guiding and protecting me. I know he is.

To those who may be struggling, never accept less for yourself than you accept for others. If you wouldn't harm, berate, punish and abuse someone else, that is evidence that you are able to show up for yourself in the same way. If that feels impossible, please investigate the beliefs and experiences that have taught you that you are worth less than others. Those wounds can be treated and mended, and you can develop self-compassion, boundaries, self-acceptance and an unshakeable inner strength.

Importantly, you don't have to do it alone, nor should you. We are stronger together. We can carry each other when we are injured, and we can heal others when we ourselves are healed.

Chapter 25

In the Spirit of Florence

Kerry Page

Rising to my work as an international humanitarian.

'You do not need to be a front-line nurse or aid worker to practise humanitarianism. You just need to put "true and loving" kindness into action.'

Where my travel bug came from, I do not know. I grew up in country Queensland in the 1950s and was sent away to boarding school, where there was little encouragement to pursue a long-term career, for most women in that era worked for a few years, married and had children. More than anything, I wanted to travel the world and have adventures. So, in the late 1960s, I trained as a nurse, not because of any altruistic motives, but to travel.

My first foray overseas was to the most popular route of my generation – England and Europe – without a care in the world! I had no insurance, there were no mobile phones or the internet, and I had not a single thought that any harm could possibly come my way.

My work with a private nursing agency in London was eventful and largely entertaining. While engaging with famous actors, nobility, and eccentric elderly patients, I was funding my trips to Europe, where my adventures included narrowly escaping being strangled by a manic-depressive lord and almost being put in jail in Spain by the Guardia Servile due to my lack of Spanish skills and an altercation over groceries. Fortunately, I was saved by a courtly English retiree who politely suggested I learn the language.

Such were the adventures that I relished because, intrinsically, I knew I was safe.

However, there was one incident in London where I was anything but safe. I was walking home early one night in autumn and heard footsteps behind me. I walked faster, as did the person behind. I looked back to see a rather harmless young man behind me, who laughed at my reaction, and then I reverted to my previous musings. Moments later, I was grabbed from behind by the same young man. He came up under my skirt, which luckily left my arms free and the ever-present umbrella one carried in London. And as I beat him over the head, he was startled, dropped his knife, and hotfooted away. I ran for home in the opposite direction, burst in the door and recounted the story to my flatmates with great hilarity over a few drinks. Then, I gave it no more thought.

However, a few days later, I was walking in a deserted lane and a stranger came out of nowhere and asked directions. The poor man was no doubt horrified when I screamed and ran off.

Many years later, I was living in Asia when a friend called me to the scene of his deceased wife. As one of the first people to arrive, I identified that she was dead and, just as I moved to the phone to call for help, I saw a large carving knife coated in blood and realised it was a murder. Immediately, in my mind, I was back on that street in London with the man who had the knife. Like classic post-traumatic stress disorder (PTSD), I then suffered from poor sleep, poor concentration, increased flight and fight response and difficulties in entering the building where I lived, due to fear.

Friends and family urged me to return home, but I wanted to stay and overcome my fear. So, I read books to learn how to deal with post-traumatic stress, continued to work – and eventually I recovered. The skills that I learnt from that experience equipped me well for my future work, and I never experienced PTSD again. While I wouldn't say I am grateful for the attack, I am grateful for the vital mental health skills that emerged from it.

My next venture took me to Haiti and Noumea with Club

Mediterranean where I worked as a nurse during the day and entertained the guests at night! Stage shows were performed by all staff every night regardless of their day job. A cashier, cook, sailor or nurse by day … a stage performer by night! During the day, I dealt with suicides, heart attacks, deaths, asthma, anaphylactic shock – with minimal medical assistance and a clientele with a propensity to sue – all in my stride. It was the stage work, however, that terrified me!

Nonetheless, this job helped to build my confidence in working as a sole practitioner outside a hospital setting and in countries with a variety of languages and health systems. With my interest in emergency health now paired with my love of travel, I ventured to Saudi Arabia in the late 1980s and spent five years working in a trauma centre where modern medicine mixed with the Bedouin life. I remember being shocked the first time I saw the son of a man, who had died in the trauma room, wrap his father in a carpet, throw him over his shoulder and walk out the front door.

When the first Gulf War broke out, the hospital became the initial point of treatment for wounded US military. Despite assuring my family that Riyad was safe, we experienced bomb alerts on a nightly basis from scud missiles that were launched from Iraq. In the early days, we would don our gas masks (for protection against chemical weapons) and take refuge in a makeshift bomb shelter comprising of a dining room table with mattresses on the top and sides, and a stock of water and cigarettes inside. After a month or so, I adapted to this environment, and when the sirens rang, I would reach for the gas mask, roll over and go back to sleep. I saw this experience as an adventure. While we were applying our expertise in an event that was being watched by the world, we forged many friendships that remain strong to this day.

With my sights now turned towards international work, I went to Asia in the early 1990s to work and study for my Masters in Public Health and Tropical Medicine. The more I learnt about international conflicts and crises, the keener I was to get involved. How grateful I am now for my nursing experiences that nurtured this passion.

In 2000, I joined the international branch of the Australian Red Cross and worked in the humanitarian field in countries in conflict for the next 22 years. One of my early missions was to South Sudan where we were based in a hospital on the Kenyan border from where we would fly into South Sudan to collect the wounded. The region was dotted with many small airfields and there was always a huge welcome when we arrived. The wounded would be loaded onboard, and despite often terrible injuries, these tall warrior-like men and women wouldn't reveal any sign of pain.

Travel in Sudan could only be done by small plane, as roads were scarce, poorly maintained, often mined, and definitely not secure. I travelled extensively throughout the South Sudan region and met remarkable health staff who worked in extremely poor conditions. One such person was a doctor whose reputation for amazing achievements spread across the country.

One day, in his small, mud-hut hospital, I watched him operate on a strong, slim woman who had been given a spinal anaesthetic and was nonchalantly lying on the operating table with her arms crossed behind her head. The windows were open, and interested family and friends peered in. Despite a complicated and extended procedure, the woman remained unperturbed, and when it was finally over, she was left to recover in the care of her daughter. By morning, she was back on her feet!

From our comfortable life in first-world countries, it is impossible to imagine what it means to flee one's home and livelihood with nothing, often losing family in the chaos and having to exist in a camp for displaced persons, with total dependence on others and little idea of what the future holds. Many people spend years in these camps waiting for relocation in their own country or a host country, while others take matters into their own hands and find ways to seek a new life in a foreign country, which is a dangerous journey. In 2009, I witnessed the challenges of displaced people in a camp of over 100,000 in Sudan, where I managed a centre for severely malnourished women and children.

Many women travelled long distances to reach the camp, often without their men and with children, and would arrive with severe malnutrition. It was devastating to see five to ten children dying in a day and to witness the grief of the mothers who had deprived themselves to give everything to their children. Sometimes, I treated children (usually around two years old) who refused to eat and would vomit any food that we managed to give them, as if they didn't want to keep living. It was often the grieving women who would wrap me in their arms and comfort me with, 'Poor foreigner, too soft.'

Indeed, my career as an international humanitarian exposed me to many traumas, which strengthened my resolve to continue the work. Each mission was marked with memorable moments, but some places, such as South Sudan and Afghanistan, remain deep in my heart. In these places, where conflicts protracted across generations, many people have never known peace, and yet they welcomed us in their country and homes and shared what they have.

It became a requirement for Red Cross staff to have a psychological assessment upon return from a mission. For many years, I would visit the same person and be assured that I was 'very normal'. He had a large clientele of military personnel who had returned from overseas postings and was interested to understand why my mental health remained stable, while many military members struggled to return to normal life. Perhaps this is partly because our missions were so different. Mine was to aid people affected by conflict regardless of what side of the conflict they were on, while the military have a combat role focused on an enemy. There are various other factors that contributed to my resilience and wellbeing.

Firstly, my early encounter with PTSD and the ongoing support and dialogue with my counsellor/ psychologist ensured that I conducted regular reflection and self-assessment. By knowing the warning signs of PTSD, I was able to manage it and prevent it from escalating.

Secondly, knowing that I could always come home was a great advantage. Unlike most people trapped in dangerous conflict zones, I had the luxury of being able to pull a lever and exit when the pressure was too great.

Thirdly, despite my poor record of maintaining contact with friends and relatives at home in Australia, I somehow managed to keep a community of friends and cannot stress how important this has been. Some travellers would say they had no desire to return home, as everyone was just doing the same thing year in, year out. This is far from my experience, as everyone's lives are evolving, and to me the permanence of others gave me the freedom to move about and the stability of knowing I had a landing base to return to.

Fourthly, it is the strong, generous and courageous people who I have lived and worked with around the world who have given me strength and resilience to endure hard times. In addition to my colleagues (the mainstay of any mission), it is the people who are 'stuck' in environments of conflict and crisis and find coping methods and strengths to continue their lives, that bring the best out of me.

Over the last 20 years, I have seen humanitarian assistance become increasingly dangerous. The nature of conflicts has changed, with terrorism being more prevalent, and the Geneva conventions and humanitarian workers no longer being respected. This results in less access to those in need, less understanding of their needs and huge restrictions in delivering the aid that is needed.

I have recently turned 70 and returned home with no plans to leave again. I am enjoying my friends and the freedom that I have been blessed to have in my home country. Many ask, have I retired, and it is a question I am unable to answer, as I know there's much more that I can do, even here in Australia.

In 2015, I was a recipient of the highest international honour for a nurse – the Florence Nightingale Medal. On the back of the medal is an inscription: '*Pro vera misericordia et cara humanitate perennis décor universalis*', which means 'true and loving humanitarianism – a lasting general propriety'.

Humanitarianism, to me, is a non-exclusive practise of valuing human life and benevolently helping others to reduce suffering and improve the conditions of humanity. You don't need to be a front-line nurse or aid worker to practise humanitarianism. You just need to put 'true and loving' kindness into action. We can all do it, every day.

Every decision we make, every path we take, has consequences. While I have missed much in the lives of the people at home – births, marriages, deaths, and special occasions – I have enjoyed a life rich in adventure and experience. It is these memories that fuel me with gratitude and happiness. If those who live in conflict and hardship can find reasons for hope and gratitude, so can we all.

Afterword

Natalie Stockdale

'Tell me the facts and I'll learn. Tell me the truth and I'll believe. But tell me a story and it will live in my heart forever.'

Native American Proverb

I'm not a mathematician. Numbers, in fact, make my eyes glaze. However, the following fact gave me pause to ponder. With each year of our lives, we bank over half a million minutes of experience.

Being a human is not simply a sum of those minutes, but rather the organisation and meaning we attach to them. In other words, the stories we create from our experiences.

Stories are a primal means to understand ourselves and the world around us. They help us to convey morality, life lessons, traditions and hope. Stories stretch back to the beginning of time and transcend cultural and geographic boundaries. Stories bind us all, Indigenous and non-Indigenous, as humanity.

Scientists explain our affinity with stories by a pair of hormones – oxytocin and cortisol – which are released when we're engaged in a story. Oxytocin is our social bonding hormone that enables us to empathise and care for the characters. Cortisol is a stress hormone, which is triggered if we perceive that the characters who we care for are threatened. The dance between these two powerful hormones explains why we are hardwired for story.

Perhaps these 'campfire' stories made your hormones dance. Did they inspire you, empower you, stretch you, challenge you, validate you, or touch you in any way?

The stories shared around this campfire offer a treasure-trove of wisdom from truly inspirational women. It has been my absolute pleasure and privilege to work with each of these women who have generously shared their stories with us, *for* us.

Without exception, every story was shared for one reason – to enhance the lives of other people. Although their experiences are vastly different, they all reflect the good and bad in their lives. By sharing their stories publicly, as they have done here, they are exposing their vulnerable selves, and *this* is an act of courage, self-acceptance, kindness and love.

In the words of author Brene Brown, 'Owning our story and loving ourselves through that process is the bravest thing that we will ever do.'

I thank every woman for the gift of their story. How consoling it is to know that we are not alone or unique in our struggles, and that there are many pathways to peace and happiness.

Equally, I am thankful to Dr Lucy Hone for kindly opening the 'campfire' with a foreword. I discovered Lucy quite by accident, but if you've read the stories in this book, you may agree that it was more a case of serendipity. While in New Zealand recently on a holiday, I met a young mother of three little boys who tragically lost her husband in a freak accident. This young mother told me that Dr Lucy Hone was a global resilience expert whose wisdom was key to her own trauma recovery.

Upon researching Dr Lucy's approach to resilience, I appreciated why she was so admired by and helpful to the young mother and countless other people who have suffered from trauma. What resonates with me mostly about Lucy's approach to healing is her 'helping or harming' question: 'Will this thought or action help, or harm me?' Whether a thought or action will help or harm our wellbeing is such a simple, yet practical tool to guide us to prudent decisions.

Years ago, before life experience turned me to the world of wellbeing, I was a Humane Educator. I would teach people, across all ages, the importance of kindness to all life on Earth – people, animals and ecosystems. Similar to Dr Lucy's 'help or harm' approach to personal wellbeing, is a principle in Humane Education of making consumer and behavioural choices that cause more good and less harm to life on our planet. It was affirming to see the same 'helping or harming' principle applied to our personal wellbeing as effectively as it can be applied to wider circles.

When we hear the stories of other people, we discover common ideas and common experiences. Sometimes we hear stories that may disrupt or debunk old beliefs and attitudes. When I first discovered Tanya Heaslip's story, for example, my own heart-sinking boarding school memories were rekindled. Although I loathed my six years at boarding school, I trivialised my experience by telling myself, *we weren't physically or sexually abused like other children, so it's not a 'real' trauma'.* Or, *it's an experience of the privileged. Who am I to complain about boarding school when other children are starving, or dodging bullets in a war zone?*

Inevitably though, the unhealed pain would sometimes creep to the surface, only to be brutally forced back down with, *shut up and be grateful.*

Immediately, however, I resonated with Tanya's story. I related to her powerlessness, her disconnection from home and everything she loved, her loss of self and the absence of kindness inside the cold walls. Tanya 'owned' her story and the impact it had on her life. By sharing it, Tanya enabled me to legitimise my own childhood story, to face my reality that boarding school *was* horrible! By bringing it into light, as Tanya has done so eloquently, we can empathise with her, acknowledge our own pain, and in turn, heal. I am grateful for Tanya for sharing her story and paving the way for others, like me, to heal their wounds and *fly free*.

Every story in this 'campfire' collection makes me proud to be human. Often through media, and sometimes through disappointing or devastating personal experiences, we can form a dismal view of humans. These women, however, share some of the best virtues of humanity, which have equipped them well to rise from, or rise to extremely tough challenges. While each storyteller faced different challenges, you may have noticed some common resilience tools that enabled them to cope and rise.

Let's explore some of these 'hero' tools.

Exercise was often used to help gain strength – physically and mentally. Margaret Cunneen took up boxing. Kate Steels *swims* around the world. Jennifer Butters *runs* around the world, and Kay Danes ran on the spot above a stinky sewage tank next to her prison block! Linda Stanley observed that her confidence grew in sync with her fitness, and of course, Liesl Tesch's sports took her on international adventures.

The benefits of exercise to our wellbeing are succinctly expressed by a former American Football coach, George Allen.

> *'A workout makes you better today than you were yesterday. It strengthens the body, relaxes the mind, and toughens the spirit.*
>
> *When you work out regularly, your problems diminish and your confidence grows.*
>
> *A workout is a form of rebirth. When you finish a good workout, you don't simply feel better, you feel better about yourself.'*

Nature was often referred to by these women as an important healing tool. Take Grace Westworth, for example, who would look for nature every day; Linda Stanley and Sandra Black, who flourish in their gardens; Kobe Steel, Ondine Sherman and Amina Abaza, who closely connect with animals; Vicki Simlesa, who needs the outdoors as much as oxygen; and Kate Steels and Jacqueline Hope, who are nourished by open water.

Given the abundance of research that shows that nature is medicine, this is unsurprising. In our modern, urban-centred world, many people have no or little connection with nature. 'Nature Deficit Disorder' is a term to describe the human costs of alienation from the natural world, which was coined by Richard Louv. Similarly, Edward Wilson refers to the 'Biophilia Theory' – that we are intrinsically connected to and a part of the natural world. When we're disconnected, we can't optimally function or flourish.

The term 'forest bathing' began in Japan. I call it – 'green fun'. Similarly, I call being in, on or looking at water (my favourite place) – 'blue fun'! Don't we always feel better after a dose of either?

Social connection is another 'hero' tool shared by most, if not all women. For example, Coralee Lever expressed how important it was for her to return to her shop after the Port Arthur massacre, to maintain her social connection with her community. When Sandy Sullivan was in the depths of despair in a refuge for women, it was the kind staff who carried her through. Although Regina Razumovskaya has suffered the horrors of war and the trauma of displacement, she cites the time when she felt alone as being the hardest experience of all. Whether it be health professionals, family, friends or community, every storyteller attributed their recovery, partly, to their connection with other people.

The clear message here is that we don't need to suffer alone, and it's 'normal' to sometimes need help. Humans are hardwired to connect with other people, to feel that we belong to a tribe, a group, to feel close to other people.

Even people who engage in 'social snacking' report greater happiness. Whenever we chat briefly with the check-out staff in supermarkets, the stranger next to us in a queue, or our hairdresser, we are social snacking and improving each other's wellbeing.

Social connection, however, is not about the number of people we socialise with, or how many Facebook friends we have. The long-term benefits come from *meaningful* connections. As some women have shared around this campfire, adversity is a good way to discover your *true* friends.

You may have noticed that there are certain character virtues common to the women around this campfire that have enabled them to rise from, or *to* their challenges. Virtues are among our most powerful allies in difficult times. As I said around the first *Campfire for the Heart* book, if we take care of our character, our character will take care of us.

Gratitude is one of the most powerful virtues that we can harness to help us overcome trauma and find happiness. Even in the darkest of places, there is always light, always something for which to be grateful. While Tamana Ashorzada was robbed of her freedom and basic human rights in Afghanistan, she still found reasons for gratitude.

Sometimes, in the depths of despair, we might require self-discipline to seek reasons for gratitude. As Ondine Sherman said, 'Sometimes this means forcing yourself to spell it out, write it down daily. I am grateful for ....' It might be the water that flows to you by simply turning a tap, or your faithful dog who wags his tail every time he sees you, or your true friends who stay by your side. If we switch on our gratitude radar every day, we will feel better.

Kindness is another virtue common to these resilient women, and it was often expressed by their acts of service to others. Indeed, sharing their stories for this book is an act of kindness in itself. While Amina Abaza, Kobe Steel, Ondine Sherman and Vicki Simlesa have devoted their lives to helping animals or their environments, many other women are committed to helping other people – Lucy Hone, Kirsty Sword Gusmão, Pip Rae, Jennifer Butters, Sally Herzfeld, Suzie Ratcliffe, Kay Danes, Sandy Sullivan, Coralee Lever, Liesl Tesch, Mia Finlay, Noelene Brown and Kerry Page, among others.

In the words of international personal development and business guru, Tony Robbins, 'the secret to living is giving'. When we help others, we become part of something that is bigger than ourselves and feel better in ourselves. When I thanked Shanna Whan (the founder of Sober in the Country) for her words of praise for my first book, *Campfire for the Heart*, she graciously replied, 'My pleasure. We're all in this together.'

I think Regina Razumovskaya, who was deeply touched by the bag of apples given to her and her family, sums up the essence of kindness. 'Kindness,' she said, 'is a gift we don't keep for ourselves. We pass it on, and it revolves around the world. Receive kindness graciously, then pass it on.'

Oceans of courage have been shown by these women.

Margaret Cunneen stood up to the powerful and formidable anti-corruption machine; Kay Danes endured torture and heinous prison conditions to maintain truth and integrity; Amina Abaza faces constant criticism and threats when she challenges animal abusers; Kobe Steele rose above her agoraphobia to travel to the jungles of Borneo, and Tamana Ashorzada ever so gently defies the dreaded Taliban regime. And, of course, few people have the courage to swim in icy waters, sail the world solo and indeed work with crocodiles and bees!

The word 'courage' evolved from the Latin word for heart – *cor*. With courage, we use strength from our heart to overcome fear. Courage doesn't mean that we are fear*less*, it means we act regardless of fear. I love the way Ondine Sherman speaks of 'shooshing' her fear as she faces her future with courage. With the virtue of courage, we stretch beyond our comfort zone and embrace new challenges, new experiences, new relationships, a new world … which may be, as Regina Razumovskaya says, thrilling!

If nothing else, the stories around this campfire may have affirmed to you that we are all a part of humanity doing the best we can to survive and thrive in a life punctuated by the unexpected. As humans, we are more the same than we are different, and despite our hardships, happiness is within our reach – if we choose it.

Every woman around this campfire has *chosen* happiness. They all said 'no' to victimhood and chose not to give up. Holocaust survivor Victor Frankl said that the last of the human freedoms is 'to choose one's attitude in any given set of circumstances, to choose one's own way.' Nothing, not even the brutal Taliban, aggressive Russian troops, devastating tragedies, or the opinions of others, can take this away from us.

Following the catastrophic Port Arthur shooting massacre, Coralee Lever articulated this attitude beautifully. 'I was determined to ensure that I would not let what I had lost ruin what I still had. I refused to become another victim.'

I liken pain and trauma to fire. If mismanaged, they can be devastatingly destructive, but if wisely harnessed, they can become fuel to rise and ultimately enrich our lives.

Although the stories shared here are abundant in resilience and sagacity, remember how far *you* have come, how you too have risen from pain and adversity.

I cannot find better words to close this campfire than those of the late Queen Elizabeth 2 – 'Let us not take ourselves too seriously. None of us has a monopoly on wisdom.'

About the Author

Natalie believes that hardships are an inevitable and essential part of life experience that shape our character and enrich our lives. How we handle our hardships is a choice.

Natalie was raised in the country and educated in boarding school and universities in Melbourne. The moment she completed her studies, she took off to the Australian outback, thirsty for adventure and freedom. After teaching in a remote Aboriginal community in the Northern Territory, 'governessing' on an outback sheep station and teaching at 'school of the air', Natalie married and, with her husband, bought a drought-stricken sheep and cattle station near Longreach, Queensland.

There, Natalie's 'resilience muscle' quickly grew through her experiences of long-term solitude, droughts, floods and raising her three daughters in isolation. She learnt the power of gratitude, nature, and relationships with people *and* animals – to restore and maintain wellbeing.

In her late thirties, Natalie discovered her love of sailing and the ocean, and created a new life with her family on the NSW coast. Suddenly, in 2009, her world fell apart- losing her marriage, family, home and business. While struggling to manage her trauma, she moved to Melbourne as a Humane Educator and, shortly after, was diagnosed with cancer.

After surviving cancer, Natalie eventually woke up to the importance of resilience for the health of our mind *and* body. She subsequently resigned from her job as CEO of the Jane Goodall Institute Australia, dived into the world of wellness and now writes inspirational books to make happier, resilient people.

www.stockdalewellbeing.com

Empowering stories of overcoming adversity

Campfire for the Heart

Stories of Resilience

Lindy Chamberlain-Creighton, Matt Golinski, Gayle Shann, Steve Parish OAM, Yarraka Bayles, Chad Staples and more ...

Natalie Stockdale

More Campfires?

We are planning to publish more 'Campfire for the Heart' books about inspiring, resilient people. Possible future titles include: Campfire for a *Survivor's* Heart, a *Man's* Heart and an *Animal Lover's* Heart.

If you have, or know someone who has an engaging and inspiring story of resilience, we invite you to email a brief summary (200–250 words) to Natalie Stockdale, **natalie@stockdalewellbeing.com**, and include your age, country and which book your story would fit.

The stories chosen for the books are curated to reflect a broad range of life challenges and resilience tools. Please understand that while we cannot publish all stories offered, every submission will be considered with sincere respect and gratitude.

Support Services
Lifeline: 13 11 14
lifeline.org.au

Suicide Call Back Service: 1300 659 467
suicidecallbackservice.org.au

Beyond Blue: 1300 224 636
beyondblue.org.au

Support for eating disorders and body image issues – Butterfly's National Helpline:
1800 ED HOPE (1800 33 4673)
www.butterfly.org.au

Limit of Liability/Disclaimer of Warranty
The content in the *Campfire for a Woman's Heart* book is for informational purposes only and is not intended as a substitute for professional advice, diagnosis, or treatment of any health condition. Always consult your qualified healthcare provider with questions regarding a condition or challenge. Never disregard professional advice or delay seeking help because of content you have found in this book. Reliance on any information provided in the book is solely at the reader's discretion and risk. You and your healthcare provider must make any final decisions as to what's best for you.